BRAZIL:
Politics in a Patrimonial Society

*The Allyn and Bacon Series
in Latin American Politics*

FEDERICO G. GIL, EDITOR

The University of North Carolina

ARPAD VON LAZAR, ASSOCIATE EDITOR

The Fletcher School of Law and Diplomacy
Tufts University

ALLYN AND BACON, INC.   BOSTON

Brazil:
Politics in a
Patrimonial Society

RIORDAN ROETT

Associate Director of the
Graduate Center for
Latin American Studies,
Vanderbilt University

LIBRARY OF CONGRESS CATALOG CARD NUMBER: 77-190029

For the Corris Sisters, especially Agnes,
and Edna, Gertrude and Josephine

Contents

Preface

In this book about Brazilian politics, I have attempted to focus on two interrelated themes. The first is the tradition of the "patrimonial" or paternal state; the second is the continuing involvement of the military in national politics since the fall of the empire in 1889. The two are interrelated in that the military, since 1964, occupy the key decision-making positions in the patrimonial order. As important, the military have played a key role in preserving the power hegemony of the patrimonial state over Brazilian society since 1889.

It is time for a major reassessment of social science analyses of Brazilian politics, especially the period from 1945 to 1964. The assertion that Brazil experimented with democracy during the 1946 Republic is clearly a too facile assessment of a complex period. That era, in my view, demonstrated both the strengths of the patrimonial order and the inherent weaknesses of the Western democratic model for Brazil.

Not all aspects of the political system receive attention in this analysis. The areas selected for discussion provide an elaboration of the main political developments in Brazil, principally since 1945, as they relate to the realities of the political system: political parties, the church, students, labor, industrial groups, and the military. These chapters are preceded by a discussion of what I term the "givens" in Brazilian politics and a very brief consideration of social, economic, and geographical factors.

My sincere thanks are due to James D. Cochrane and Robert T. Daland for reading and commenting on an earlier draft of the manuscript. In addition, Jaime Garcia Reis, Steven Arnold, and William Gallagher offered helpful comments and suggestions on specific aspects of my work. Naturally, the interpretation of Brazilian politics presented here is my responsibility alone. Translations into English — except where a translator is cited — are also mine.

R.R.

1

A Nation of Regions: The Physical and Social Setting

The functioning of the Brazilian political system is influenced by important nonpolitical determinants. These provide, over time, a framework within which the configurations of power emerge that characterize various regimes in Brazil. Among the most important of these determinants are the nation's geography, the distinctive regional bias in national settlement patterns, the demographic aspects of national growth, and educational and social developments. Each of these has contributed to the shaping of the present political system of Brazil.

GEOGRAPHY

Brazil occupies approximately 47 percent of continental South America. Its 3,287,195 square miles make it the fifth largest nation in the world (only the Soviet Union, Canada, China, and the United States are larger).

The largest portion of Brazil is composed of highlands. The only significant plain areas are in the South along the Western border where the lowlands of Paraguay extend into Brazil and in the upper Amazon Basin where the lowlands of the Andes Mountains in neighboring Spanish America extend into territorial Brazil. Unlike the Western coast of South America, Brazil has

1

no significant mountain ranges. The highest elevation, that of Pico de Bandeira, Northeast of Rio de Janeiro, is about 9,500 feet above sea level.

The Brazilian highlands are best characterized by the Great Escarpment, a steep slope, difficult to climb, that gives the appearance of a mountain range when viewed from the sea. The escarpment is most pronounced from the state of Bahia southward to Rio Grande do Sul. In the area of the cities of Rio de Janeiro and Santos, the escarpment is more than 2,500 feet high, and mountain ranges about 7,000 feet in elevation are not uncommon.

The Doce River and the Paraíba River valleys are the only significant breaks in the escarpment. And in just two locations, between Santos and São Paulo in the state of São Paulo, and between Paranaguá and Curitiba in the state of Paraná, does the escarpment provide a suitable opening to the ocean.

The geography of Brazil is further fragmented by the rivers which drain the Brazilian highlands. They all flow to the ocean over steep falls and rapids, which seriously impede navigation. Only the Amazon River is navigable any distance into the interior. The Paraná river system flows westward into the interior; the headwaters of the Uruguay River flow westward also, turning south only at the Argentine border. These, combined with the other rivers of the central-south, drain southward to the River Plate system in a circuitous fashion.

The rivers which drain to the north pose similar problems for transportation and navigation. The São Francisco River originates north of Rio de Janeiro and follows the coast for more than a thousand miles before veering eastward in Bahia toward the Paulo Afonso Falls and finally reaching the Atlantic Ocean. The monumental tributaries of the Amazon Valley, the Tocantins-Araguaia, the Xingú, and the Topajóz, all flow northward and descend over falls and rapids to reach the Amazon.

Poor river navigation has impeded the physical settlement and political organization of Brazil. The barrier posed by the escarpment hindered easy penetration of the Brazilian interior by early settlers and has provided a continuing challenge for the construction of port facilities. The major concentrations of population and commercial and industrial activity have grown up in spite of, and not aided by, the topography and river system. Another important factor influencing settlement patterns was the high quality of the soil along the coastal plain. The production of sugar, cacao, and coffee, among other crops, flourished in the reddish clay soil of the coast. The natural advantage in agriculture, combined with the obstacles to interior colonization, determined the location of the bulk of the population along the relatively narrow coastal strip.

CLIMATE, VEGETATION, AND MINERAL RESOURCES

The climatic variation experienced in Brazil, situated almost wholly in the torrid zone, ranges from the highly humid, equatorial regions centered in the Amazon valley and the Northeast coast to the frost zones of the three southern states. The irregularity of rainfall in the Northeast region (most of the area receives between 20 and 25 inches a year compared to an average of more than 80 inches elsewhere in Brazil) has created severe economic and social problems which will be examined later. While climate does not necessarily determine settlement patterns, it does influence the distribution of population. Thus, about 90 percent of the nation's people are concentrated in the relatively overpopulated coastal and southern zones.

The Amazon basin and the coast from Bahia south is covered by a tropical rain forest; the Southeast and São Paulo state are heavily forested also. The Brazilian interior is covered with a mixture of forest and grassland. These areas range from the scrub woodland to vast stretches of savanna to open grasslands with little forestation. The interior Northeast, an irregular rainfall zone, is characterized by drought-resistant trees known as *caatinga*.

Brazil possesses one of the world's largest and highest quality iron ore reserves, most of which is located in Minas Gerais. Manganese, copper, lead, zinc, nickel, chromium, quartz crystal, and industrial diamonds are to be found also. Coal is the most important mineral lacking. The only deposits are in the south and are of poor quality. The high ash content makes it unsuitable for producing coke. The hydroelectric power potential is enormous and is speedily being developed. Recent discoveries of petroleum off the Northeast coast hold out the possibility for eventual self-sufficiency in that crucial product. The nation has succeeded in combining many of its resources to create the world's nineteenth largest steel industry (5 million tons in 1970) centered at Volta Redonda. The government's goal is to produce 20 million tons by 1980, to place it among the top ten steel-producing nations in the world.

Only in recent years, then, has Brazil begun to mobilize its vast store of natural resources for modernization purposes. The possibilities of industrialization and great power status will depend in good measure on the effectiveness with which the Brazilian government is able to link human and natural resources efficiently with national development goals.

REGIONS AND REGIONALISM IN BRAZIL

The diversity of Brazil is exemplified by its regions; each represents a particular aspect of the cultural, historical, economic, and ethnic diversity of the whole. The unity of Brazil has often seemed superficial, and, indeed, in colonial times "Brazil" was little more than a loosely connected series of coastal settlements. The first decades of the empire, after independence from Portugal in 1822, were spent in repressing separatist movements in the Northeast and South. While the empire provided a central focus for national unity, the power and influence of the regions remained a fact of life in the nineteenth century.

The highpoint of regionalist autonomy came with the Old Republic (1889-1930). The federal government served as little more than a clearing house for regional political and economic decisions. The Vargas era (1930-1945) saw a steady diminution in the influence of the states and regions. It was in 1932 that the last dramatic separatist movement, that of São Paulo, threatened to destroy Brazilian unity. That effort received little sympathy from other regions, and federal troops defeated the rebels.

The 1946 Republic (1946-1964) saw a compromise with the regional phenomenon. The states were granted some

Table 1
REGIONS OF BRAZIL

| Principal Regions of Brazil | Area (km²) | % of Area | Population | | % of Total Population |
			1960	1970 (Estimated)	
NORTH States—Acre, Amazonas, Pará Territories—Rondônia, Roraima, Amapá	3,581,180	42.07%	2,601,519	3,518,000	3.67%
NORTHEAST States—Maranhão, Piauí, Ceará, Rio Grande do Norte, Paraíba, Pernambuco, Alagoas, Sergipe, Bahia	1,548,672	18.20	22,428,873	27,304,000	31.60
SOUTHEAST Minas Gerais, Espírito Santo, Rio de Janeiro, Guanabara, São Paulo	924,935	10.86	31,056,432	41,473,000	43.76
SOUTH Paraná, Santa Catarina, Rio Grande do Sul	577,723	6.79	11,873,495	18,042,000	16.73
CENTRAL-WEST States—Mato Grosso, Goiás Federal District	1,879,455	22.08	3,006,866	4,968,000	4.24
BRAZIL	8,511,965	100.00	70,967,185	95,305,000	100.00

Source: Anudrio Estatístico do Brasil — 1969.

autonomy, but the powers of the federal government, on balance, outweighed the combined force of the states. Since the Revolution of 1964, the central government has effectively curbed any show of independence emanating from the state government. The centralization of power in Brasília is quite clearly the trend.

FEDERALISM

The centrifugal force of regionalism accounts for the federal system of government in Brazil. The federalist principle accommodated the individuality of the several regions, and their component provinces or states, while preserving the core unity of the nation. Federalism has served as a general framework within which the administrative and political goals and social and economic demands of the states have been dealt with without causing the disintegration of national unity. That unity has been achieved often at the cost of decision-making effectiveness at the center.

For a country possessing grave economic and geographic disparities, a federal system was an apt one — particularly in view of the fact that other emerging societies (most notably the United States), with similar disparities, had adopted federalism. But federalism is not a logical, institutional outgrowth of the peculiar socioeconomic realities that have shaped Brazil. Moving from a unitary form of government during the colonial period to a centralized bureaucratic empire in the nineteenth century, Brazil's first four hundred years were spent exclusively under the domination of an authoritarian state. Even under the decentralized Old Republic (1889-1930), the states of the federation had little of the independence and personality such units possess in other federal systems. They remained dependencies of the central government, the weaker leaning heavily on their stronger regional neighbors.

The goal of the majority of the states is less to define and consolidate their role in the federation than it is to use their influence with the federal government to increase their share of the goods and services it dispenses. Given the glaring economic disparities among the states, the federation appears as the only hope for income redistribution and the stimulation of economic development via state intervention and subsidies.

Federalism in Brazil, from the beginning, has been a dependent federalism. The country is a federation of economically unequal partners all beholden to the dictates of the state. The latter found federalism to be a subtle device for administrative and political organization as well. In a country the size of Brazil, possessing such enormous geographic and economic differences, federalism provided a relatively simple solution for the central government to the challenge of national unity and political control, if not national integration, particularly in the eighteenth and nineteenth centuries.

In a truly federal order no sovereign exists. But regardless of the period in Brazilian history we analyze, the federal system has been subordinate to the political domination of the state. The states have had meaning in Brazil only insofar as the political objectives of the national government have required it. Federalism has not been a "process by which a number of separate political communities enter into arrangements for working out solutions, adopting joint policies and making joint decisions on joint problems."[1] Brazilian federalism has not been characterized by joint and mutual deliberation. Nor has the dialog taken place among relatively equal communities — in either the political or the economic sense.

LOCAL GOVERNMENT

The present condition of the Brazilian federal system can be examined by briefly considering state and municipal government. Both levels have been dependent financially and politically on the central government in varying degrees for decades; this dependency has increased since 1964.

The states are granted the power to create their own constitutions and government, normally parallel to the central government. Between 1946 and 1964, the governor was popularly elected; since 1965 gubernatorial elections have been

[1] Carl J. Friedrich, *Trends of Federalism in Theory and Practice* (New York: Frederick A. Praeger, 1968), p. 7.

indirect, and the popularly elected state legislative assemblies select governors. The states tend to assume only those constitutional powers that the federal government declines to execute, although the 1946 Constitution reserved to them all powers not included in the broad grant of powers given to the federal government. The 1967 Constitution contains similar provisions. In areas such as education and interstate traffic, the states have concurrent power with the federal government, but state legislatures may only supplement existing federal law and in no way conflict with it.

The 1946 and 1967 Constitutions allow the federal government to intervene in the states to repel invasion, suppress civil war, reorganize finances, insure the execution of judicial orders, maintain national integration, and preserve the separation of powers in the state governments. Before 1946 intervention was common. Between 1946 and 1964 intervention was a rare occurrence. The threats of the Goulart government to intervene in Guanabara State in 1963 were motivated by the antipathy of the national government toward the outspoken criticism of Governor Carlos Lacerda, a leading opposition figure. The maneuvering of both state and federal governments filled headlines for months, but the Goulart government failed to carry out its threat to intervene. After 1964, and especially from 1964 to 1967, the military government intervened at will to fulfill its program and root out political opponents.

The predominance of the federal government is due to its economic power and its assumption of greater and greater responsibility in providing public and social services. The major sources of revenue are reserved in the Constitution for the federal government. The states may levy taxes on sales, inheritance, transfers of real property, and exports. The sales tax normally provides 60 to 70 percent of state revenue. Federal aid to the states, along with the omnipresent offices and programs in the states of the federal bureaucracy, increases state dependence on the central government. Between 1946 and 1964, the federal government was often late in fulfilling its obligations to share certain revenues with the states. Since 1964, the federal government has been careful to utilize its economic influence to control the development plans of the states to be sure they have been in accord with national goals.

The position of the states has been described as follows:

> The majority of member-States live today on federal budget apportionments, not sustaining or even maintaining their own administrative machinery, growing more and more inefficient every day, uselessly duplicating public services furnished by the Union or by municipalities, and thereby restricting their possibilities of development, because the State has pre-empted their economic and financial resources, in the same way as the Union has done to the States. In many of them, besides voting the budget, the entire work of the costly legislative assemblies, during their entire session, is restricted to partisan political discussions or to the voting of projects related to the governmental bureaucracy.[2]

As originally introduced into Brazil by the Portuguese, the municipality had to serve both urban and rural interests. Given the magnitude of the colony and the predominantly rural nature of its population, local institutions "became centralized politically and decentralized geographically. . . . The Brazilian colonial municipality remained in a somewhat primitive stage as a community and was highly ineffective as a unit of government."[3]

While the Constitution of 1824 explicitly supported municipal autonomy, real authority remained with the central government of the Empire, which acted through the appointed chief executives of the provinces. Until 1889 little interest was shown in strengthening local government. After the collapse of the Empire in 1889, the municipalities still found themselves dominated by the state governments. The Constitution of 1891 and the federal system it represented provided little room for municipal independence. The Vargas years, except for the short-lived period under the Constitution of 1934 (1934-37), saw both state and municipal government overwhelmed by the central government. There was no room for independent action by any level of government, except the national, under Getúlio Vargas.

---

[2] Quoted in Diogo Lordello de Mello, "Administrative Decentralization and the Brazilian Municipal Reality," in Ivan Richardson (ed.), *Perspectives of Brazilian State and Local Government* (Los Angeles: International Public Administration Center, School of Public Administration, University of Southern California, 1965), p. 24.

[3] Frank P. Sherwood, *Institutionalizing the Grass Roots in Brazil: A Study in Comparative Local Government* (San Francisco: Chandler Publishing Co., 1967), p. 34.

With the downfall of Vargas in 1945 and the Constitution of 1946, a three-level system of government was instituted. The document is often referred to as a municipalist charter because of the determined effort to stipulate municipal autonomy carefully. Article 28 stated that local officials would be elected at the local level; that local needs would determine municipal administrative organization; that flexibility in the administration of local services was in order; and that the municipality would have independent sources of revenue and the right to spend its income as it saw fit.

While the 1946 Constitution acknowledged three levels of government, it did not specify the powers of the municipality. As a result, the jurisdictional lines between levels of government remained blurred. It soon became apparent that the states would again overwhelm the municipalities because of the specific powers given to state government to create new municipalities, specify their areas of jurisdiction, and supervise their administrative and fiscal activities. Moreover, the revenues that were to be shared among levels of government infrequently materialized. The sources of revenue open to the municipalities were grants-in-aid from the national government; locally generated revenues, such as taxes on land, buildings, real estate transfers, and business and professions; and shared revenues. The 1946 Constitution provided that the central government was to share with municipal governments taxes on oils and combustibles, electric energy, minerals, income, and excise taxes. New taxes were to be shared as well. When the state tax collections in any municipality exceeded the total income of the local unit, 30 percent of the excess had to be returned. But both the federal and state governments were delinquent in sharing funds with the municipalities: "Payment of the municipal share of the vital income and excise taxes became a cruel farce."[4] Diverse reasons led the state and federal governments to renege on their constitutional responsibilities to share revenues. The pressure of inflation increased, and available funds were needed for state and federal programs; the quota

[4] Ivan L. Richardson, "Municipal Government in Brazil: The Financial Dimension," *Journal of Comparative Administration*, Vol. 1, No. 3 (November, 1969), p. 328.

payments required legislative action, and they were often delayed by the political instability of the 1946 Republic; the long history of fiscal malfeasance by municipal officials made the authorities reluctant to "lose" additional, scarce resources; and since the large cities received little of shared revenue, they saw little reason to fight on behalf of smaller municipal units.

With the 1964 coup d'état, the situation of the municipalities did not improve. The 1967 Constitution made few alterations in the types of revenues to be shared. The state sales tax was to be shared for the first time, but the excess tax sharing was cancelled. Twenty percent of the federal taxes on income and industrial production was divided equally between states and municipalities. Two control mechanisms were created: a State and Federal District Participation Fund and a Municipal Participation Fund. These two funds allow the central government to audit the municipal expenditures in a close and continuing manner, since all shared funds were administered by the two units.

In late 1968, following a major political crisis in the military regime, the earlier period of new and increased funding ended. Over the next two years the amount paid to each fund was reduced, as was the amount of income and industrial taxes slated to be shared with the funds. With Constitutional Amendment No. 1 in October 1969 and the succession of General Médici to the presidency, further centralization occurred and the municipalities found themselves facing an uncertain future once again.

The mayors and members of the Brazilian municipalities are elected directly except for the executives of the most important cities, who are appointed by the state governors. This is to assure that the major cities will be administered by supporters of the government party. An interesting political repercussion of the indirect election of the governors is the potential growth in importance of the mayors. As the most visible popularly elected state officials, the mayors may well attempt to capitalize on the fiscal independence the resources of the two funds provide, if and when the central government is willing to release the promised funds.

THE REGIONS

The attempts to classify the regions of Brazil are myriad. We shall utilize here the standard categorization of the Brazilian Institute of Statistics which identifies five major regions: the North, Northeast, Southeast, South, and Central-West.

The North

Possessing 42 percent of the federal territory, the North encompasses the states of Amazonas, Pará, and Acre and the territories of Rondonia, Roraima, and Amapá; it contains only 3.6 percent of the national population. The North is dominated by the Amazon valley. The population, largely seminomadic, is of mixed European-Amerindian blood, and more than 60 percent of this population is located in the state of Pará. Economically the region serves the export market by supplying forest products, primarily rubber, nuts, lumber, and fibers. Since the rubber boom of the first decade of the century, the North's contribution to the national economy has been the lowest of all the regions — about 2 percent.

The North gained new prominence in the early 1970s with a surge of interest by the military regime in its development. Continuing neglect of the Amazon was seen as a potential threat to national security; the Program of National Integration, announced by President Médici in 1970, called for the building of a trans-Amazon highway which would allow for the penetration and settlement of the area.

The Northeast

The Northeast is the oldest of Brazil's regions. It was the site of the first permanent settlement and, during the sixteenth and seventeenth centuries, set the cultural and economic standards of the colony. Its political influence continued long after its economic decline into a dependency of the more dynamic south in the late nineteenth and twentieth centuries.

Comprised of nine states of Maranhão, Piauí, Ceará, Rio Grande do Norte, Paraíba, Pernambuco, Alagoas, Sergipe, and Bahia, the area represents 18.2 percent of the national territory and contains 31.6 percent of the population. Most of that population is concentrated along the coast.

The Northeast is divided into three distinctive zones. The fertile coastal strip was the area of original settlement in Brazil. Dominated by large sugar plantations, its most recent fame came from the attempt, in the early 1960s, to organize Castroite peasant leagues. The leagues attempted to challenge the social and political hegemony in the region of the wealthy *usineiros* or sugar producers. The Northeast figured prominently in the politics and planning of the 1946 Republic with the creation of SUDENE — Superintendency for the Development of the Northeast, led by the economic historian Celso Furtado.

The *agreste*, an intermediate zone behind the coastal strip, is characterized by small subsistence farms whose produce is primarily for the local market. While the coastal zone receives plentiful rain enabling it to cultivate sugar, the *agreste* receives regular but less plentiful rainfall.

It is the interior zone of the Northeast, called the *sertão*, that is the semiarid area subjected to periodic droughts and extreme variations in patterns of rainfall. It is an area of high temperature and inferior soils. Characterized by cattle raising and subsistence agriculture as well as by cotton, it is this zone that is included in the drought polygon established by the federal government to give special consideration to the area in time of extended drought. The attention of the government, beginning in the 1950s, has been directed at reducing the growing disparity between the economic development of the Northeast and the Center-South — without a great deal of success.

Each of the three zones holds a distinctive ethnic group. The coast received large numbers of African slaves in the heyday of the sugar cycle; these, along with the European descendants, occupy the area along the coast. Blacks, Europeans, and Amerindian strains mingle in the *agreste* to produce a distinctive racial type. The *sertão* population is predominantly

Amerindian-European in composition. While these groups are characteristic of each of the three areas, increased mobility and migration as well as continuing miscegenation among the groups blurs the distinction more and more with each decade.

The Northeast, then, is the most traditional and historical of Brazil's region. It is today a depressed area economically, more rigid socially than the rest of the country, and conservative in its politics, reflecting the continuing influence of the landed oligarchy and their cohorts. It is subject to severe climatic variation and has received sporadic and dramatic attention from the federal government in an attempt to resolve the basic problems of overpopulation, high unemployment, and illiteracy.

The Southeast

Comprised of the states of Espirito Santo, Minas Gerais, Guanabara, Rio de Janeiro, and São Paulo, the Southeast represents 10.8 percent of the national territory and has 43.7 percent of the nation's population. It is the economic center of contemporary Brazil. Much of the mineral wealth of the nation is found in this area, as is the industrial complex that has come into being since 1930. The Southeast accounts for the nation's iron and steel production, the manufacture of consumer and capital goods, and the textile industry. Industrial, commercial, and cultural activities are centered in the major cities of this region — Rio de Janeiro, Belo Horizonte, and São Paulo. In addition, much of the administrative and political decision-making remains concentrated in Rio de Janeiro, the former federal capital before the capital moved to Brasília.

The growth of the Southeast is reflected by rapid urban expansion and in the sprawling slums that encircle its cities. While urbanization and slums are characteristic of the Northeast regions as well, they have attracted more attention and have assumed far greater proportion in the Southeast. The region dominates the educational system, serving as a magnet to attract people from all over Brazil who seek employment and a new life. It is in this region that political activity is concentrated.

The South

This region is made up of the states of Paraná, Santa Catarina, and Rio Grande do Sul. It is an area of temperate climate and of basically European settlement, being the most European of the several regions. Paraná is the leading coffee-producing state in the federation (coffee represents a little more than 50 percent of national exports). The three states are important agricultural and livestock centers. Its people appear to be more aggressive and dynamic than their counterparts in the Northeast; the society and culture are somewhat more egalitarian, suitable for the frontier background of these states that border on Spanish America. Containing 16.7 percent of the population, the Southeast occupies 6.7 percent of the national territory. It is the home of a significant number of national political leaders, ranging from Getúlio Vargas to the incumbent president, General Médici.

The Center-West

This region contains the federal district of Brasília and the states of Goiás and Mato Grosso — 22 percent of the territory and 4.2 percent of the population of Brazil. The Center-West is the area of future development in Brazil. Somewhat reminiscent of the frontier of the United States, it is an area of low population density, extensive cattle ranches, and agricultural productivity geared for the urban markets of the south and east. The area is rich in minerals such as tin and titanium, chromium, manganese, and nickel. It is a region of rapid population growth.

The decision to build the modern city of Brasília on the plateau of the Center-West testifies to the vision of change that gripped the nation's leaders in the 1950s. The West looms large in the national consciousness as the interior, as an area to be conquered and integrated into the nation. While its political role is marginal — comparable to that of the North — its potential is far greater, considering the demographic changes taking place.

The Significance of Regionalism

Given the distinctive patterns of colonization, settlement, and economic growth during the colonial period — which were accompanied by the accumulation of social influence as well as of economic wealth by the predominant families of the regions — regionalism became and remains a potent variable in discussing politics.

Regionalism is a phenomenon accepted without hesitation in Brazil. Not only is each of the five regions a distinctive variant of the national culture but also the economic development of each has contrasted remarkably with the others. Each of the regions, and the states which they encompass, illustrates the tremendous diversity of the Brazilian federation and helps to explain the calculated use of the federalist principle by the autonomous state in its effort to dominate and control the nation-state. Through combinations of the most powerful states in each region and the antagonism among regions and states, the national political elite has effectively diluted the potentially disruptive influence of regionalism and made it a fairly docile instrument of its own control. The most dramatic failure of this operating principle, the 1930 revolution, serves as an excellent case study of this phenomenon at work.

In each region one or two states predominate. This pattern, established early in Brazilian history, holds true today. The smaller, unequal members of the federation have remained peripheral, dependent entities; the predominance of four or five states remains an actuality. One way in which the state — and a sign of its flexibility and subtlety — has prevented political revolt by the smaller, and usually forgotten, entities has been by the absorption and co-option of potential leaders from these areas. The federal bureaucracy, the military, and the congress have been the main outlets for these individuals who would seek to redress the imbalance in Brazilian federalism. Thus, a need for new manpower is satisfied while the erstwhile rebellious leaders find themselves comfortably absorbed at the center by the state.

In the Northeast, it is the states of Pernambuco and Bahia that are preeminent; in the Southeast, São Paulo and Minas Gerais; and in the South, Rio Grande do Sul. At various times and in different combinations these states have determined the course of political events. It is from these states that the nation's political leadership comes. The interests of these states and these three regions structure the internal dynamics of the Brazilian state.

During the Empire the Northeast played a major role in national politics. With the advent of the Old Republic in 1889 São Paulo and Minas Gerais came to occupy the principal position nationally; and after 1930 Rio Grande do Sul succeeded in winning a position of national importance. Today these states — along with Guanabara, the former federal district — remain the most influential.

DEMOGRAPHIC AND SOCIAL DATA[5]

The population of Brazil is estimated at 93 million (1970), making it the eighth most populous nation in the world. The population growth rate is estimated at 2.8 percent annually, which is lower than Colombia, Ecuador, Peru, and Paraguay (3.4 percent) but higher than Uruguay and Argentina (1.2 percent and 1.5 percent respectively). The population density per square mile in 1970 was estimated at twenty-eight compared to eleven in Bolivia, thirty-three in Chile, and twenty-three in Argentina. In 1970 55.9 percent of Brazil's population was classified as urban; in only three other countries on the continent was a smaller proportion of the population designated as urban — Ecuador (46 percent), Paraguay (36 percent), and Bolivia (29 percent). In 1970 61.5 percent of Brazil's population five years and older were classified as literate; the figure for

---

[5] Data in this section are taken from *Atualidade Estatística do Brasil* (Rio de Janeiro: Fundação IBGE, 1969); *Anuário Estatístico do Brasil* (Rio de Janeiro: Fundação IBGE, 1969); *Statistical Abstract of Latin America* (Los Angeles: Latin American Center, University of California, 1969); *Socio-Economic Progress in Latin America*, Annual Reports of the Social Progress Trust Fund of the Inter-American Development Bank, 1965-1970.

those ten years and older is 67.9 percent. This means that more than one-third of the national population five years and older is illiterate (38.4 percent), and the figure is 32 percent for those ten years and over. These figures represent a national estimate and obscure the vast differences between rural and urban areas. Only Bolivia (39.8 percent in 1968) had a lower percentage of national literacy.

A new effort to eradicate illiteracy was begun in 1970 with the creation of the MOBRAL (Brazilian Literary Movement) campaign. The first emphasis has been on the fifteen- to thirty-five age group. The effects of the national movement are being felt very slowly.

Life expectancy at birth in Brazil is estimated to be 65.4 years (1970), with only Bolivia (53), Ecuador (55), and Peru (55) having a lower expectancy in years. The infant mortality rate (per 1,000 live births) is estimated at 92, with only Bolivia (108) and Chile (100) having a higher rate. The daily caloric intake per capita, in 1967, was 2,690 calories, the fourth highest on the continent, surpassed only by Argentina, Uruguay, and Chile. The Gross National Product per capita in 1968 was estimated (U.S. dollars) at $240, with only Paraguay ($200), Ecuador ($190), and Bolivia ($160) being lower.

Brazil has one of the highest growth rates of urbanization in South America: 2.3 percent. Only Colombia (3.0 percent) and Peru (2.4 percent) are higher. From 1950 to 1960 the growth rate of the total urban population in Brazil was 5.5 percent; it was 5.2 percent in cities with 20,000 and more in the censuses of that period and 7.8 percent in the last census. Between 1920 and 1960 the urban population (in cities of 20,000 or more) increased from 11.3 percent to 28.1 percent.

The rate of population increase in the smaller and newer cities in Brazil (and six other Latin American nations) exceeds the rate of growth of the total urban population and that of the older, established cities. While Brazil is rapidly urbanizing, it does not share a common characteristic of the other nations in Latin America: the concentration of more than a third of the urban population in one city (Montevideo 46 percent, Buenos Aires 34 percent). São Paulo and Rio de Janeiro, cities of more than a million inhabitants, have only 12.8 percent of the national population. The Social Progress Trust Fund Report

(1968) estimates that Brazil will have eight cities with a population of more than a million by 1980.

Brazil's educational situation remains among the more underdeveloped in Latin America. In 1969 only 52 percent of the five to fourteen age group were attending primary school; on the continent, only Colombia (49 percent) had a lower figure. The government of Brazil announced in 1968 that primary education would be compulsory for all school age students in the country's urban centers, but this has not been effectively implemented as yet.

Secondary students, as a percent of the fifteen-nineteen age group, was 37 percent in the late 1960s (Bolivia and Colombia 33 percent, Chile 28 percent, and Paraguay 21 percent). In the overall average of students as a percent of the five-nineteen age group, Brazil had a rank of 48 percent, with only Colombia ranking lower (45 percent).

In 1968 there was a total enrollment of 259,000 students at the higher level, of whom 61 percent were in universities. The remaining enrollment was in independent centers of higher learning which lacked university standing in accordance with established legal requirements. There was a total of forty-eight universities in Brazil in 1970, twenty-five of which had been created between 1955 and 1965. Fifteen of those twenty-five had been established by the federal government. Of the students matriculated at the beginning of the academic year in 1968, 152,164 of 278,295 students were enrolled in universities in three states of the Southeast: Minas Gerais, São Paulo, and Guanabara.

It is estimated that 52.6 percent of the population in Brazil is less than twenty years of age, which further over-burdens the antiquated education system. In order to meet the needs of this growing population, greatly increased investment in teacher training, school construction, and educational materials is needed.

As Table 2 shows, income distribution in Brazil favors the wealthier groups, as it does in all of Latin America. Six percent of the population in Brazil receives 51 percent of the national income, the highest percentage of the five countries considered.

These figures, in comparing Brazil to the other countries in South America, hide the wide disparities among regions in

Table 2
SELECTED INCOME DISTRIBUTION ESTIMATES*

Country	Poorest 20% Population	30% below Median	30% above Median	15% below Maximum	Richest 5% Population	Richest 1% Population
Argentina	5.2	15.3	25.4	22.9	31.2	16.3
Brazil	4.2	12.6	24.4	...	33.0	18.0
Colombia	5.9	14.3	23.1	...	30.4	10.0
Mexico	3.6	11.8	26.1	29.5	29.0	16.5
Venezuela	3.0	11.3	27.7	31.5	26.5	16.0

Source: Statistical Abstract of Latin America, 1968, p. 19.
*Figures refer to percent of total national income.

Brazil. The imbalance between the Northeast and the Center-South, particularly, has been aggravated in recent decades. The South and the Southeast contained 50.4 percent of the population in 1960, although these regions represented only 17.6 percent of the national territory. The Northeast has been in a period of relative decline since the end of the nineteenth century; its share of the population has fallen from 46.7 percent in 1872 to 31.6 percent in 1960.

In 1967 a national index of 11.8 deaths per 1000 inhabitants included rates of 15.7 and 9 in the Northeast and South respectively. In the same year, infant mortality, nationally, was recorded at a rate of 93.3 deaths per 1000 live births. However, in the Northeast, the index was 133.8 deaths and in the South, only 71.4. Life expectancy at birth estimated for 1968 at between 56 and 58 years for the country as a whole, was between 62 and 64 years for São Paulo and Guanabara, and from 49 to 51 years for the Northeast.

As Table 3 demonstrates, the Northeast lags economically behind the South.

The problem of literacy continues to plague the Northeast as well, as Table 4 demonstrates.

This very brief summary of some social and demographic indicators of Brazilian development illustrates the challenge confronting any government in power, military or civilian. The major accomplishment to date of the military regime has been its superior economic performance. In 1965-1969, total gross

Table 3
COMPOSITION OF WORKERS BY WEEKLY SALARY – 1968

Salary (NC$) (5 cruzeiros equals $1.00)	Workers		Paraná, Santa Catarina, Rio Grande do Sul
	Northeast	São Paulo	
Less than 30	74%	40.8%	50.3%
From 30 to 60	15.8%	32.8%	34.0%
More than 60	10.2%	26.4%	15.7%

Source: SUDENE: Dez Anos (Recife: SUDENE, 1969), p. 196.

Table 4
PERCENT OF LITERATE PEOPLE 6 YEARS AND OLDER – 1968

Area	Northeast	São Paulo	Paraná, Santa Catarina, Rio Grande do Sul	Minas Gerais, Espirito Santo
Urban	68.6	82.5	83.9	76.4
Rural	35.8	68.8	68.6	51.5
Region or State	49.0	78.1	74.9	62.8

Source: Same as Table 3, p. 198.

production grew at an average annual rate of 6.0 percent, equivalent to a per capita growth of 2.7 percent a year. After very high growth in the early 1960s, the rate of increase in total output fell to 1.5 percent in 1963 and rose to 3.6 percent in the 1964-1966 period, under the military government's strict policy to curb hyperinflation. Public policy encouraged growth after 1967 and, by official government data, gross domestic product (GDP) increased 8.4 percent in 1968 and 9.0 percent in 1969. The 1970 rate of growth followed the 1969 figures closely. Table 5 shows the comparative growth rates in GDP for South America and Mexico.

The record of Brazil under the present regime has also been impressive in manufacturing output: Brazil showed an average increase of above 10 percent for the 1966-1969 period. The regional average for Latin America was 7.2 percent. Of the total value of Latin American manufacturing production in

1966-1969, Brazil, Argentina, and Mexico accounted for about
75 percent.

Table 5
ANNUAL GROWTH RATES OF GDP

Country	1961-65	1966-69	1966	1967	1968	1969
Argentina	2.9	4.5	0.2	2.3	4.7	6.6
Bolivia	5.9	6.1	7.0	6.3	7.2	4.8
Brazil	3.1	7.4	5.1	4.8	8.4	9.0
Chile	4.7	2.9	7.0	2.3	2.7	3.5
Colombia	4.6	5.2	5.4	4.2	5.5	5.8
Ecuador	4.8	5.5	4.6	6.5	5.2	4.9
Mexico	7.7	7.2	6.9	6.3	8.1	7.3
Paraguay	4.7	5.2	1.3	6.7	4.8	4.2
Peru	6.1	2.5	5.7	4.6	1.4	1.7
Uruguay	0.3	-0.1	3.3	-6.6	1.2	5.5
Venezuela	7.9	4.3	2.3	4.0	5.3	3.5
Latin America	4.9	5.7	4.5	4.4	6.3	6.5

Source: Inter-American Development Bank, *Socio-Economic Progress in Latin America,* Social Progress Trust Fund, Tenth Annual Report, 1970, p. 2.

The agricultural record has been less satisfactory. As Table 6 demonstrates, Brazilian production has barely kept ahead of Latin America and suffered a reverse in 1969.

In the context of population growth, Brazil faces a

Table 6
ANNUAL GROWTH RATES OF PHYSICAL AGRICULTURAL PRODUCTION

	Total Production			Per Capita Production		
	1961-65	1966-69	1969	1961-65	1966-69	1969
Brazil	4.4	2.7	0.6	1.4	-0.3	-2.4
Regional production						
All products	2.6	2.3	1.4	-0.2	-0.5	-1.4
Food products only	3.1	2.5	0.7	0.3	-0.3	-2.1

Source: Same as Table 5, p. 28.

continuing problem of foodstuffs supply for its people in both the rural and the urban zones. The agricultural question is directly related to the issue of structural reforms: Will the Brazilian government act with authority to redistribute national income to raise the standard of living in the countryside? Related to this is the question of agrarian reform — access to land for small farmers. In addition, productive capital in sufficient amounts for crop cultivation and land improvement is required. An effort must be made to stimulate the formation of local capital. The voluntary mobilization of rural savings, in the opinion of the Inter-American Development Bank, "should provide a major portion of the increase in funds for agricultural credit in Latin America."[6] The bank has identified two areas that require attention if the Brazilian economy is to maintain its high rate of performance. The first "is to shift the industrial development strategy from an almost exclusive reliance on import substitution to one based on accelerated production for both domestic and export markets. Further expansion of these markets will depend on raising productivity and reducing costs and prices."[7] The second major challenge, according to the analysis of the bank, "is to increase rural output, employment and income."[8]

Economic growth for what? — that is the pertinent question for the military regime in Brazil. Will they use the impressive economic performance of the late 1960s and early 1970s to provide social justice as well as increased popular participation in national affairs for all Brazilians? Or will the fruits of progress be shared among only a narrow sector of the population?

Brazil confronts a number of development bottlenecks that must be dealt with in order to facilitate future change. An outdated educational system, an antiquated land ownership tradition, sprawling urbanization, underemployment, a mediocre level of agricultural production, high levels of illiteracy and infant mortality, and regional imbalance — these, and others, will require attention in the immediate future.

[6] *Socio-Economic Progress in Latin America* (1970), p. 88.
[7] Ibid., p. 131.
[8] Ibid.

SUMMARY

While Brazil is one of the five largest nations in the world, we have seen that more than 90 percent of its population lives in three regions — Northeast, Southeast, and South — that represent less than 35 percent of the national territory. The North and the Central-West remain outposts of Brazilian civilization.

The geography of Brazil poses serious difficulties for national integration. The river systems do not provide natural linkages between the regions. The Great Escarpment poses a real barrier to easy port development. The nation's natural resources, while potentially abundant, are largely untapped, and Brazil lacks one important ingredient for a self-sustaining industrial complex: coal.

National unity has been seriously compromised by the distinctive regions of Brazil. The five regions, but particularly the Northeast, Southeast, and South, represent unique patterns of development. The federalist principle provides a flexible and workable mechanism for political and administrative organization, but the growing disparities between the Northeast and the South raise serious policy questions for the federal government.

Brazil is undergoing rapid urbanization as part of the modernization process. The movement from rural to urban centers is one of the highest in Latin America. But the country still remains heavily rural and agricultural. Indices of social welfare indicate a position far inferior to many of Brazil's smaller neighbors. The challenge of twentieth-century growth is to mobilize the nation's economic resources effectively to satisfy social needs through effective political leadership. The demographic, geographic, and social impediments we have explored in this chapter indicate the magnitude of the challenge confronted by the political system. Not only do these determinants indicate the enormity of the problem, they also help to shape the growth and differentiation of political roles in the society. Chapter 2 examines the various phases of political development in Brazil, with primary emphasis on the period following 1946. It is during the last twenty-five years that successive social and economic crises have posed a continuing challenge to the Brazilian political system.

2
The Brazilian Political System in Perspective

INTRODUCTION

There are certain basic assumptions that underly this study of the Brazilian political system. These are "givens" in that they serve as independent variables, dominant over time and relatively immune to change from outside the system itself. It is the purpose of this chapter to explore the most important of these independent variables and to illustrate their significance historically. They provide a framework within which we can assess the roles of institutions and socioeconomic groups in a political context. Among the most important of these are the concept of elite rule, the maintenance over time of a patrimonial regime, and a low level of national integration.

Among the leading attributes of the Brazilian political system is its elitist nature. Regardless of the time period, politics in Brazil have been dominated by a relatively small group of individuals who have been able to manipulate the mass of the population and define the goals of the state in their own terms. Most members of the elite have been drawn from groups such as the landowning oligarchy, the public bureaucracy, the export-oriented and commercial interests, the military, and the industrial and banking groups. The elite nature of the political system has been reenforced by the traditional and hierarchical nature of Brazilian political culture. Through history there has been a high degree of similarity and congruence in the political ideas, attitudes, and action patterns of the elites. Similarly there has been a notable lack of opposition to this prevailing political culture by other groups and classes in Brazil. Emerging social groups have chosen to emulate existing elites and their code of political conduct rather than to challenge or confront them.

Elite domination is further aided by the oft-noted propensity for compromise and the peaceful settlement of disputes among elite members and the expectation among the masses that accommodation and bargaining are sufficient to settle disputes:

... few persons who know Brazil will deny that the forms of domination elaborated by the groups who have traditionally held power ... and in large part continue to do so have been singularly effective in mitigating and controlling violent social conflict .... in no other country in Latin America do such staggering inequalities (material, social, political, racial, and regional) seem so little productive of individual tensions and resentments or of intransigent, regimented collective strife.[1]

What has emerged in Brazil is a pattern of elite interaction that assigns great value to pragmatism in policy-making, displays little ideological fervor, endorses flexibility in interpersonal relationships, and stresses highly personal or charismatic forms of leadership.

The elitist nature of politics has been accompanied by the existence of a centralized, bureaucratic state which has served as an effective weapon for the continuation of the influence of the Brazilian elites. Raymundo Faoro in *Os Donos do Poder* refers to the transfer from Portugal and the re-creation in Brazil of a "patrimonial regime" that succeeded in dominating and directing the economic and social development of the colony.[2] The patrimonial regime gained new vigor during the empire and continued to dominate Brazil during the periods of the Old Republic and the Vargas era. (See Table 7 for a breakdown of periods of government.) Confronted for the first time by a potentially viable alternative during the 1946 Republic, repre-

[1] Frank Bonilla, "Rural Reform in Brazil," *American Universities Field Staff Reports,* Vol. 8, No. 4 (October 1961), East Coast South American Series (Brazil).
[2] Raymundo Faoro, *Os Donos do Poder* (Rio de Janeiro: Editôra Globo, 1958).

Table 7
BRAZIL: HISTORICAL PHASES OF THE PATRIMONIAL REGIME

I.	Colonial Period, 1500-1822
	1. Rule from Lisbon, 1500-1808
	2. Rule from Rio de Janeiro, 1808-22
II.	Empire, 1822-89
	1. Peter I, 1822-34
	2. Regency, 1834-40
	3. Peter II, 1840-89
III.	Old Republic, 1889-1930
	1. Military/Civilian Oligarchy, 1889-98
	2. São Paulo-Minas Gerais Hegemony, 1898-1930
IV.	Transitional Republic (The Vargas Era), 1930-45
	1. Provisional Government, 1930-34
	2. Constitutional Government, 1934-37
	3. *Estado Novo* (dictatorship), 1937-45
V.	1946 Republic, 1946-64
	1. Presidential Government, 1946-61
	2. Parliamentary Government, 1961-63
	3. Presidential Government, 1963-64
VI.	Military Republic, 1964-Present
	1. Controlled Government, 1964-69
	2. Authoritarian Government, 1969-Present

sentative democracy, the patrimonial regime demonstrated its resiliency during the crisis of 1961-1964; the military coup of March 31, 1964, confirmed the continuing power of the patrimonial regime against all challengers.

In the few instances in Brazilian history when a major segment of the national elite has been eliminated — in 1930 when Vargas assumed power and in 1964 when the Armed Forces seized control of the government — the basic structure of the patrimonial order was not disturbed. The coming to power of Vargas or the military merely meant that different members of the elite were to occupy key decision-making positions. The administrative bureaucracy continued to function, as did the spoils bureaucracy; both were merely in different hands. In both instances the new figures were drawn from both the military and the civilian sectors of the elite. The new holders of power had been members of the national elite but without primary responsibility for governance within the system. With the change at the top, one subset of leaders was replaced by another. Although they might differ on specific policies, they did not disagree on the basically elitist nature of the political system and the necessity of retaining the patrimonial order as a means of preserving their own status.

The 1964 military coup is noteworthy because of the efforts of the armed forces politically to neutralize leaders of the ousted elite by depriving them of their political rights for ten years. This unprecedented step reflected a decision to eliminate permanently elite members thought guilty of having broken the rules of the game while in power by having tried to incorporate nonelite groups into the political system.

Our use of the term *patrimonial* refers to the creation and maintenance of a highly flexible and paternalistic public order, dedicated to its own preservation and the preservation of the unity of the nation-state, whether under imperial, republican, or military tutelage. The patrimonial state in Brazil is first and foremost a bureaucratic state in that the authority of public order is maintained by the administrative apparatus of the central government. As Robert Daland has pointed out, the bureaucracy is divided in two, between a technically oriented, "civil service" segment (the *técnicos* or planners and technical experts, often economists) and the "spoils" bureaucracy that is utilized by the ruling elite to reward friends, to co-opt potential and actual political opponents, to satisfy local and regional allies, and to deal with newly emerging social groups in order to build support for the system.[3] It has been estimated that in 1920, one out of every 195 actively employed Brazilians was in the federal bureaucracy. By 1940 it had become one out of every 132, and by 1960 it was one out of every 65. It appears quite clear that this trend has continued since 1964.[4]

The bureaucracy and the bureaucratic mentality are all-pervasive in Brazil. They reflect the prevailing political milieu in which a heterogeneous national elite has had to construct an adaptable political mechanism for governing a nation in which regional and local power centers continue to compete for

[3] Robert T. Daland, "Development Administration and the Brazilian Political System," *Western Political Quarterly,* Vol. 21, No. 2 (June, 1968), 325-39.

[4] Philippe C. Schmitter, *Interest Conflict and Political Change in Brazil* (Stanford: Stanford University Press, 1971), p. 33.

influence. The patrimonial order survives and flourishes because the collective interests of the elites provide sufficient incentive to overcome factionalism. The patrimonial order stands as a composite term for many of the attributes noted by other students of Brazilian politics. Its enduring success depends upon what Philippe Schmitter has termed corporatism:

> . . . a belief in and acceptance of a natural hierarchy of social groups, each with its ordained place and its own set of perquisites and responsibilities. These "orders" have and accept voluntary restrictions on their autonomy and horizontal interaction. They are seen as linked by vertical lines of subordination directly to higher social institutions, which are conceded the right and the duty to intervene in intergroup conflicts for the sake of social peace.[5]

It encompasses the concept of *clientelismo,* a system of decision-making that is based on an exchange of substantive favors, legal privilege, or protection from punishment among political actors; Anthony Leeds's *cabide de emprêgo,* literally an "employment hanger" that represents an organization or a single individual who holds more than one position;[6] *empreguismo* signifying co-optation through public employment opportunities for one's followers and/or opponents; the *Estado Cartorial* or "sinecure state" of Hélio Jaguaribe in which public employment serves as a means of co-optation and political control;[7] and the System (*"O Sistema"*) analyzed by James Rowe. It represents the several elites which have dominated Brazilian political machinery during several successive governments and their pattern of joint action to maintain control and preserve "social peace" through heavy reliance on conciliation and paternalism.[8]

The literature is replete with these and other concepts and terms which attempt to capture the style and content of the

[5] Ibid., p. 98.

[6] Anthony Leeds, "Brazilian Careers and Social Structure: A Case History and Model," *American Anthropologist,* Vol. 66 (1964), 1321-47.

[7] Hélio Jaguaribe, "The Dynamics of Brazilian Nationalism," in Claudio Veliz (ed.), *Obstacles to Change in Latin America* (New York: Oxford University Press, 1965), pp. 162-87.

[8] James W. Rowe, "The 'Revolution' and the 'System': Notes on Brazilian Politics," Part I: Seeds of the "System," *American Universities Field Staff Reports,* Vol. 12, No. 3, (July, 1966), East Coast South America Series (Brazil), p. 7.

Brazilian political system. The term *patrimonial state,* as used by Raymundo Faoro, is more appropriate, I believe, because it conveys a more comprehensive image of politics and *society* as they are found in Brazil today. The term has the advantage of focusing on the national political system and its continuation over time regardless of the changing composition of the several political elites who fill the chief decision-making roles. The concept emphasizes the qualities of centralization and authority. It summarizes the absence of mobilization in the political system and the consensus among the elites on limiting popular participation. The patrimonial state may be "modernizing," as it has become under President Garrastazu Médici, or it may be "preservatory," as with President Dutra in the late 1940s.

The patrimonial regime reflects the profoundly rural society that Brazil was until the mid-twentieth century. The majority of the population lived outside the cities, and the greater part of these people were illiterate. Low levels of social mobilization and little effective organized interest group activity resulted. Brazil was a static society in which little changed, in terms of power relationships, over time. Only after 1946 did the social mobilization process become a significant phenomenon in national politics — but without really challenging continued elite domination.[9]

Finally, Brazilian society is characterized by a low level of national integration which aids the continuing, disproportionate influence of the few. In the absence of a truly national identity shared by all Brazilians, power is distributed very narrowly. In part, the slowness of the process of national integration is due to the size and complexity of Brazil. But it is also due to the perception of the nation held by the elite. Integration, and the formation of a truly national identity, have been neither

[9] Karl W. Deutsch, "Social Mobilization and Political Development, *American Political Science Review,* Vol. 60, No. 3 (September, 1961), 493-514. Deutsch defines social mobilization "as the process in which major clusters of old social, economic and psychological commitments are eroded or broken and people become available for new patterns of socialization and behavior." The social mobilization concept is not to be confused with social *mobility,* the capacity of an individual to move up or down the social status ladder. There was, without doubt, social mobility in Brazil because of the cyclical pattern of economic growth and the diversity of regional colonization. Those who had moved up socially and were potentially disruptive were co-opted into the existing structure of power in the society.

necessary nor desirable. To hasten the creation of a national community would be to endanger the degree of control the elite exercises with relative ease and low political cost. Thus, it is sufficient to talk about "Brazil" as though it is a homogeneous entity, while fully realizing that economic and social inequities, abetted by physical distance, preclude the formation of an integrated, national community in the immediate future.

Brazilian politics, then, must be understood in terms of a political elite which has been able effectively to dominate national politics regardless of changes in government. Elite domination has been accompanied by the growth of a powerful, centralized government — the patrimonial regime — that has effectively bypassed the federal, representative structure of the contemporary political system. Low rates of social mobilization precluded unmanageable demands until the late 1950s; and the slow rate of industrialization, in addition to the way in which Brazil industrialized, prevented the growth of autonomous interest groups with an identifiable political role in politics. The low level of national integration prevents sustained, responsible participation in national politics and further insures the continuation of the patrimonial regime and the limited political elite.

The following, brief historical sketch of Brazil is followed by an analysis, in greater detail, of the significance of these variables and their relevance for contemporary politics.

THE HISTORICAL SETTING
— THE COLONIAL PERIOD

Discovered in 1500 by the Portuguese, Brazil was ignored for the ensuing thirty years. In 1530 a colonizing expedition, financed by the Crown, set out for the new colony and established São Vicente in 1532 (modern-day São Paulo). The Portuguese monarch divided the Brazilian coastline into fifteen hereditary captaincies that extended inland from the coast as far as the colonial boundaries. Within each captaincy, the *donatario,* the individual who had received the donation from the king, assumed responsibility for colonization and financial underwriting in exchange for broad powers of governance and profit-making possibilities The only two captaincies that were relatively successful were São Vicente in the Center-South and Pernambuco on the Northeast coast. By 1549 the Crown determined to establish a central government, at Bahia, and the first governor-general arrived to assume direction of Brazil.

As agents of the Crown, the *donatarios* were the first instruments of state capitalism in Brazil. Their land was assigned by the royal government, their rights and prerogatives defined by the king, and their economic and social functions were seen as complementary to and supportive of the interests of the monarch. The Crown attempted to assert its right to regulate and stimulate, for its own advantage, the development of the Brazilian colony.

The autonomy of the *donatarios,* forcefully argued by Gilberto Freyre and others, represented local license, personal arrogance, and understandable confusion as the settlement process became routinized.[10] The authority of the landowning elite would survive the challenge of the Portuguese government until 1808 and the arrival of the royal court in Brazil. The importance of the years preceding that event, for the emergence of the patrimonial regime, was that the formal claims of royal sovereignty were never rejected outright. The superstructure of legal and administrative mechanisms required to govern Brazil was created during this period even though it was not fully legitimated in the eyes of *os poderosos.*

With the arrival of the governor-general, the patrimonial regime received its symbolic head. While the governor-general represented the power of the Portuguese throne, 250 years of conflict between mother country and colony ensued before the patrimonial state became permanently ensconced in Brazil. During the first hundred years, roughly from 1550 to 1650, the magisterial bureaucracy represented the claim to authority of the Crown. It attempted to represent the interests of the central government without stifling the vital initiative of the settlers. This magisterial bureaucracy was the historical antecedent for the contemporary, administrative bureaucracy of Brazil.

[10]Gilberto Freyre, *The Masters and the Slaves* (New York: Alfred A. Knopf, 1964).

By 1650, when Portugal had won its independence from Spain, with whom it had been forcibly united in 1580, the Crown began to cancel all concessions previously given to individuals. The fiscal interests of the Crown became the paramount determinant of public policy toward Brazil. Stimulated early in the settlement period by brazilwood and sugar, the Crown's determination to impose its rule on the colony increased with the discovery of gold in Minas Gerais in 1695. The period of unbridled hegemony in public by *Os Poderosos* (the influentials') affairs was curtailed with the assertion of royal prerogative. While the autonomy of the landowners survived — as it does today in the Northeast and West — it did so increasingly because their interests began to coincide with the goals of the monarchy. Profit became the greatest single force in Portugal's colonial policy and served to overshadow disputes about jurisdiction and administrative influence.

The society that emerged in the seventeenth and eighteenth centuries was one divided between the littoral, or coast, and the interior. The coast, dominated by the commercial class, the bourgeois merchants, aligned with the public bureaucracy, the agents of the monarchy, to direct public affairs. The interior, the reserve of the patriarchal figures that Freyre enshrines, remained under the jurisdiction of the local oligarchy.

Local and private initiative played an essential role in exploring the far reaches of Brazil — the *bandeirantes* (pathfinders), who used São Vicente as their headquarters, opened the interior of the country. Although the royal government was never far behind and often served to guide the initial ventures,[11] it must be said that the local elite was the final, determining factor in the success or failure of such ventures in the vast, sprawling colony. The Portuguese Crown was aware of the rival forces at work in the colony: increasing bureaucratic centralization on the one hand and the drive for autonomy at the regional and local level on the other. This theme survived the Colonial Period and structured the political process throughout the Empire and the Old Republic.

As part of its claim to preeminence in policy-making, the Crown co-opted the local landowners into the colonial system

[11]Richard M. Morse, *The Bandeirantes* (New York: Alfred A. Knopf, 1965); and Vianna Moog, *Bandeirantes and Pioneers* (New York: George Braziller, 1964).

through the bureaucracy. Public positions were utilized by the royal government to begin to gain the adherence of the great families of the interior as well as the bourgeois class of the coast. Sons and nephews were incorporated into the state apparatus in exchange for the loyalty and support of the landowning families. As the agricultural producers became more and more dependent on the commercial bankers and traders of the coast, their reliance on the state grew. The Crown supported the coastal groups against the pretensions of the interior. The period until 1822 and independence saw a continuing rivalry among landowners and bureaucrats and commercial interest.

During this early period, there was little demonstration of nationalism in Brazil. Ironically, the Portuguese Crown viewed the colony as an integrated unit while its inhabitants continued to identify with their region or province. The effort to centralize authority by the Crown, while allowing local and regional variation, produced a flexible situation that allowed for continuing local autonomy and the assertion of the royal position, in contrast with the rigidity and formalism of Spanish rule.

By 1750, with Pombal as the king's chief minister, the formal centralization of royal rule began to prove successful. In 1759 Pombal expelled the Jesuits from the Portuguese Empire; with their departure the traditional Church, an arm of the Portuguese settlement process, settled back into a supportive but nonparticipant role. With the transfer of the colonial capital to Rio de Janeiro in 1763, the early regional predominance of the Northeast declined; and the center of gravity in the colony began to shift, permanently, to the Center-South.

In 1789, the *Inconfidência,* an attempt by intellectuals in Minas Gerais to declare Brazil an independent republic, failed; the ringleader, Tiradentes, was executed in 1792. A last vestige of colonial administrative autonomy, the separate state of Maranhão in the North, had been eliminated in 1775. The "special relationship" of the Portuguese and the British for trade and commercial purposes, had been extended to Brazil as early as 1703; by the end of the eighteenth century England had a virtual monopoly over the colony's trade. The Crown and the colony benefited from the protection of its fleet and goods by the British Royal Navy.

At the end of the colonial
seventeen administrative captain
bishoprics of the Roman Cath
were united. Two high courts,
other at Bahia, provided a rudi
towns had circuit judges for lo
had a treasury commission to c
Crown. Local town councils, in
exceptions, dependent on the w
governor-general.

By independence, the reg
during the early years remained
corresponding social stratifical
system of the Northeast had be
a mining industry in gold and p
cattle-raising economy appeare
The social and economic orde
remained separated but comple

INDEPENDENCE AND

The Portuguese court, d
armies in 1808, settled in Rio
regent on behalf of his incap;
ports to world trade for the
ing and commercial enterp
restriction. Brazil's first print
of surgery was created, and
commercial treaty with En
commercial dominance of the

The Portuguese patrimo
its bureaucracy merged with
the three predominant socia
racy, the merchants and the
immigrants, who manned t
landed group against the oth
in Pernambuco in 1817 was
the competing groups. The
with the help of the British f

Rio Grande do Sul and raged until 1845 when it was defeated. Other revolts broke out during the decade in many of the provinces; some were republican in intent, others were in protest over local issues.

Faoro identifies two institutions that provided a modicum of stability during the 1830s as the regency struggled to keep the nation together.[12] The first was *A Sociedade Defensora da Liberdade e Independencia Nacional* (The Society in Defense of Liberty and National Independence), created in May 1831, which fought against the federalist clubs. It came to play the role of an unofficial council of state, favoring the retention of the monarchy and a strong central government. The other was the *Guarda Nacional,* or National Guard, also created in 1831, which gave the government an armed force, apolitical, loyal and able to defend the interests of the Crown — against the traditional armed forces if necessary. The regency actually downgraded the army in favor of the National Guard, which was much more its creature.

It became apparent by 1840 that the regency had not functioned very well; the unofficial experiment with republican rule had failed. The Interpretive Law of 1840 ended the experiment with federalism which had begun in 1834 with a series of constitutional amendments known as the Additional Act. Peter II's majority was declared, although he was not yet eighteen, and he assumed the throne. He ruled Brazil until 1889 and the advent of the Republic.

By 1845, the Marques of Caxias had ended the *Farroupilha* revolt in the southern provinces. The political rivalries of the empire were played out by two amorphous political parties, the Liberals and the Conservatives, both drawing their members from the same social and economic class. Under the strong tutelage of the Crown, the patrimonial state asserted itself in Brazil. The public bureaucracy carried out state policy with the pliant support of both parties and the small, literate part of the population who were aware of public policy. The honors and appointments of the monarchy assured continued support for the center from the periphery. The court, acting through the national bureaucracy, determined policy with little more than

[12]Faoro, *Os Donos do Poder*, pp. 152-54.

formal consultation with the landed oligarchy and no concern for the wishes of the rest of the population. The domination of the center continued to structure and dominate Brazilian society through the nineteenth century.

In one of the Empire's few foreign adventures, the 1865-1870 war of the Triple Alliance (Brazil, Argentina, and Uruguay) against Paraguay, the armed forces became politicized. From 1870 until the military coup that ended the Empire in 1889, the military were increasingly involved in public affairs. The two political parties of the empire competed for the support of military officers; the military buildup for the war against Paraguay provided an organizational structure ready and able, for the first time, to fight for the institutional prerogatives of the armed forces.

In addition to disaffection among the officer corps, the emperor lost the support of the landed aristocracy by the last decade of the Empire over the use of slavery. The first slaves had been brought to Brazil in the mid-sixteenth century. They provided the labor for the flourishing sugar plantations of the Northeast coast. By 1800 the slaves represented nearly 50 percent of the population. Abolition gained strong support from the British in the eighteenth century, who, because of their influence in trade and commerce, were able to lobby effectively for an end to slavery.[13] The movement toward slave emancipation had proceeded slowly in Brazil. The slave trade had been abolished formally in 1850; in 1871 the Law of the Free Womb freed all children born to slaves; and in 1885 a law freed all slaves at the age of sixty. With the Crown supporting these reforms, the landowning aristocracy felt betrayed as its economic and social eminence decreased. The Golden Law of 1888 abolishing all slavery without compensation was the final break between emperor and landed and commercial elites.

The Crown lost the support of some elements of the Church, as well, over the issue of Freemasonry. The court had taken a conciliatory position against the demands of the Vatican and the Brazilian bishops that the movement be stamped out. A Republican Club appeared in Rio de Janeiro in 1870, and the first Republican Manifesto was issued.

[13]Richard Graham, *Britain and the Onset of Modernization in Brazil, 1850-1914* (Cambridge, England: Cambridge University Press, 1968), chapter 6.

Thus, by the 1880s the traditional sources of support for the monarchy were weakened seriously.[14] Many members of the aristocratic oligarchy were less than enthusiastic about the accession to the throne of Peter II's daughter, Isabel, and her unpopular French husband. In addition, the emperor himself had lost much of his personal prestige by his seeming inability to direct national affairs with more acumen; there were rumors that he had become senile. The empire fell in a bloodless coup on November 15, 1889. Marshal Deodoro da Fonseca, an army hero, headed the provisional government. The overthrow of the monarchy was the work almost exclusively of the military.

THE OLD REPUBLIC (1889-1930)

The armed forces, aware of their corporate strength after 1870, acted in 1889 to assert their institutional influence. The break with the patrimonial regime of the Empire signified the creation of a new force, related to and supportive of the central government but able and willing to challenge and control it when deemed necessary. While the Old Republic — from one perspective — represented a victory for decentralization and the landed aristocracy, it also signified, more meaningfully, the continuation of oligarchical rule. The levels of popular political participation did not increase. The groups that had occupied prominent positions in the Empire did so during the Old Republic. The patrimonial state remained the dominant influence in the development of Brazil.

The two most influential groups from 1889 to 1930 were the military and the state governors. The armed forces dominated the Old Republic from 1889 to 1894, when the first civilian was elected president.[15] The military were never far from politics and power in the Old Republic. Marshal Hermes da Fonseca, with the backing of the political machinery of Rio Grande do Sul, served as president from 1910 to 1914.

[14]C. H. Haring, *Empire in Brazil* (New York: W.W. Norton and Company, 1958), pp. 144-56.
[15]June E. Hahner, *Civilian-Military Relations in Brazil, 1889-1898* (Columbia: University of South Carolina Press, 1969), esp. chapter 7.

The national leadership came primarily from the powerful states of Minas Gerais and São Paulo in the framework of the Republican Party, the only national party organization. The *política dos governadores* (politics of the governors) was an agreement among state leaders that granted the São Paulo and Minas Gerais axis preeminence in national affairs, particularly economic, in exchange for a guarantee to the smaller states that the central government would not interfere in internal state affairs. The co-option of recalcitrant political leaders continued. The sons of the establishment were given public employment in the bureaucracy as part of the tacit understanding between political center and periphery. The Republican Party was, in fact, a loose network of provincial organizations that served to funnel patronage into the states and provided candidates for the bureaucracy of the patrimonial state.

Civilian and military factions in the Old Republic competed for the privilege of exercising the prerogatives of the bureaucratic state.[16] Regional and local leaders vied for favors from the central government. The economy remained firmly based on coffee, a commodity heavily subsidized by the government.[17] Social stratification remained rigidly hierarchical. Political opposition to the establishment was either co-opted or brutally crushed. Representative government, the supposed core of the 1891 Constitution, was a fiction, and politics remained the game of the few in the service of the patrimonial state.

The Constitution of the Republic mirrored the western liberal democratic model of government without the substance. It provided for twenty states — coterminous with the provinces of the Empire — and a federal district in Rio de Janeiro. Significant prerogatives were reserved to the states, allowing them to construct their own administrative and tax structures in conformity with their diverse regional differences. The federal government had three branches. The legislature contained two houses, a senate representing the states, and a chamber of deputies elected on the basis of population. The executive consisted of a powerful presidency with cabinet ministers

[16]José Maria Bello, *A History of Modern Brazil, 1889-1964,* translated from the Portuguese by James L. Taylor (Stanford: Stanford University Press, 1966).

[17]Warren Dean, *The Industrialization of São Paulo, 1880-1945* (Austin and London: University of Texas Press, 1969).

responsible only to the chief executive. The judicial branch was made up of a Supreme Court and lower courts. It was a constitutional structure ideally suited to the Old Republic in which the franchise was limited, voting remained low, literacy encompassed a small percentage of the population, and social mobility was rare. The national population remained passive, objects of the political machinations of the few. An individual's loyalty was given to his *patron* or his state or region before the nation.

THE TRANSITIONAL REPUBLIC
(THE VARGAS ERA) 1930-45

The Old Republic fell when the bargain among the state governors over the presidential succession collapsed in 1930. The Paulista president, Washington Luís, refused to endorse the presidential candidacy of the governor of Minas Gerais and, instead, supported a fellow Paulista as his successor. The opposition candidate, Getúlio Vargas of Rio Grande do Sul, was backed by many young military officers, the *tenentes* (lieutenants) who had launched a series of unsuccessful rebellions against the Old Republic throughout the 1920s, the small states (Vargas's vice-presidential candidate came from Paraíba in the Northeast), and Minas Gerais. After losing the election, and with the assassination of former vice-presidential candidate João Pessôa, the forces behind Vargas's Liberal Alliance revolted in October 1930. Weakened by the 1929 economic crash, repudiated by its former political supporters, the Republic regime acceded to the counsel of the armed forces and the Church and resigned. Vargas became provisional president in November 1930.

The Transitional Republic, dominated by Getúlio Vargas, is divisible into three distinct periods.[18] The first encompasses the provisional government from 1930 to 1934. During this time Vargas moved to revise and modernize the economy. He put down regional revolts against the centralization of state

[18]John W. F. Dulles, *Vargas of Brazil: A Political Biography* (Austin and London: University of Texas Press, 1967).

power in Pernambuco and São Paulo in 1932. Delegates elected in 1933 wrote a new constitution in 1934 and elected Vargas to his first presidential term.

From 1934 to 1937, the second period, Vargas ruled within the 1934 Constitution. He successfully manipulated and defeated all potential political opponents. A communist uprising in 1935 gave him justification to suppress the party and its leader, Luís Carlos Prestes. The only other organized political movement, the fascist *Integralistas* led by Plínio Salgado, was suppressed soon after. Under the pretext of maintaining law and order, Vargas decided to ignore the 1934 constitutional ban on his succeeding himself. He abolished all political parties, canceled the 1938 presidential elections, and promulgated, with the 1937 Constitution, the *Estado Novo,* or New State. The third phase of Vargas's rule included the years from 1937 to 1945.

Executive authority was greatly expanded under the New State. The president was empowered to rule by decree, and Vargas chose not to convene the legislative assembly, thus avoiding any potential check on his unlimited power. He intervened in the states, replacing recalcitrant governors with men who would do his bidding. The central bureaucracy, in the absence of any check by an elected parliament, assumed its traditional role of creator and implementor of public policy. Extensive nationalization of economic institutions and natural resources increased the power of the patrimonial state. The ban on all organized political activity and strict censorship allowed the government to monitor public affairs with relative ease.

An opportunist rather than a totalitarian ideologue, Vargas did not organize a party to inculcate Brazilians with a particular set of beliefs. His paternalistic interpretation of his role led him to use his position to consolidate his influence with the urban working class. An extensive welfare system, the first labor unions for the privileged urban working class, elementary education programs, and public health programs were all gifts of the state to the people. In return the state expected compliance and no popular expectations of political involvement in decision-making. This represented the purest patrimonial tradition in Brazil.

In 1943 a secret but widely circulated *Manifesto Mineiro,* written by politicians in the state of Minas Gerais, called for a return to democratic government. The Brazilian Expeditionary Force, sent to Europe in 1944, returned home in 1945. The military officers supported presidential elections; their interest in reopening the political system coincided with a growing demand by the political elites for an end to the authoritarian New State.

The election which Vargas scheduled for December 1945 initiated a period of intense political debate. When it appeared that Vargas might subvert the 1945 elections, as he had those of 1937, the military issued an ultimatum. In October 1945 the dictator left for his home in Rio Grande do Sul after his unceremonious ouster by the armed forces.

THE 1946 REPUBLIC

The elections took place as scheduled, with General Eurico Gaspar Dutra, Vargas's minister of war, defeating former *tenente* Brigadeiro Eduardo Gomes, for the presidency.[19] Dutra was the candidate of the Social Democratic Party (PSD) and received the endorsement of the Brazilian Labor Party (PTB). Both parties had been organized by Vargas before his abrupt withdrawal from politics. [The UDN (National Democratic Union) endorsed Gomes.] While the political system of the 1946 Republic expanded to thirteen parties, these three remained preeminent.

The fourth party in electoral strength, the Social Progress Party (PSP), centered in São Paulo, was a personalist party created to satisfy the presidential ambition of Adhemar de Barros, a populist politician in the Vargas tradition.

In the four presidential elections held from 1946 to 1964, the PSD-PTB coalition triumphed in three: with Dutra in 1945, Vargas in 1950, and Juscelino Kubitschek in 1955. Jânio Quadros, the victor in 1960, backed by the UDN, resigned in 1961, and PTB leader João Goulart, then vice-president, became chief executive. Thus, the PSD-PTB "System" of co-option and

[19]Thomas E. Skidmore, *Politics in Brazil, 1930-1964: An Experiment in Democracy* (New York: Oxford University Press, 1967).

cooperation dominated national politics after 1946. While the number of people voting increased substantially, their relationship to the political system changed very little.

Francisco C. Weffort and others have termed this period one of populist politics.[20] Characterized by an emphasis on the urban electorate, with little, if any, tendency to institutionalize linkages between voter and government, concerned not about programmatic but pragmatic interests, the populist politician sought votes only to gain public office. Once successful, the populist used his position of influence not in the service of the electorate or the "public good," but in the narrow, parochial sense of satisfying his "clientele" or political following. A populist politician represents clients who are able to "deliver" the popular vote needed for election. To maintain this arrangement, the politician must have access to payoffs: jobs, contracts, rewards, etc., which only the bureaucracy and central government can provide. In return it is tacitly understood that he will not attempt to introduce real structural changes or to disturb the equilibrium of power between the central government's preeminence in policy-making and its clients nationally. The system functions as long as each participant understands and accepts the "rules of the game." Anyone who does not is either co-opted into the system, and his challenge rendered futile, or he is ostracized by being defeated, ignored, or belittled.

The principal "power contender" during this period was the armed forces. Given the tentativeness of the fragile electoral system, and its unrepresentative nature, the military became constant participants in politics. Their intromission was due to a number of factors which included an interpretation of their constitutional duty calling for political involvement when civilian politicians had failed to govern properly, institutional security which appeared challenged in the 1961-1964 era, and the personal ambition of individual officers. In every presidential election of the 1946 Republic, at least one military man ran as a candidate. In 1945 two military men stood for office, as we have seen. In 1950 Getúlio Vargas successfully defeated

[20]Francisco C. Weffort, "O Populismo na Política Brasileira," in Celso Furtado et al., *Brazil: Tempos Modernos* (Rio de Janeiro: Editôra Paz e Terra, 1968), pp. 49-75.

Brigadeiro Gomes, again the UDN candidate. In 1955 Kubitschek triumphed over General Juarez Távora, another former
tenente. In 1960 Quadros defeated Marshal Henrique Teixeira
Lott.

As important as the military presence in presidential
elections was their intervention in national politics. There were
military coups in 1954, 1964, an attempted coup in 1961, and
the beginnings of a coup in 1955 that brought about a
countercoup by another military faction in defense of the
constitutional regime. As we will see in chapter 6, these
military interventions were accompanied by growing dissent
among the military themselves over the appropriate role of the
patrimonial state in the modernization of Brazilian society. The
segment of the military and the civilian political elite favoring
radical reform was clearly defeated with the coup d'état of
1964 that sent President Goulart into exile.

The 1946 Republic was characterized by high rates of
social mobilization, an expanding urban electorate, populist
politics, a weak multiparty system, growing military politicalization, and a continuation of the guiding hand of the patrimonial
state in preventing reforms that would unbalance the carefully
structured distribution of power that favored the continuing
preeminence of the public sector in policy formation.

THE MILITARY REPUBLIC,
1964 – PRESENT

The fragmented, drifting 1946 Republic fell before a
military coup as had the Empire, the Old Republic, and the
Transitional Republic of Getúlio Vargas. Once again, very
limited civilian-political participation characterized the determination of the military to oust the incumbent, constitutional
regime.[21] The Military Republic, initiated in 1964, can be
divided into two segments. The first encompassed the years
from 1964 to 1969, the period of General Humberto Castello
Branco's government and that of General Arthur da Costa e

---

[21]Riordan Roett, "A Praetorian Army in Politics: The Changing Role of the
Brazilian Military," in Riordan Roett (ed.), *Brazil in the Sixties* (Nashville:
Vanderbilt University Press, 1972).

Silva. During this period the 1946 Constitution was modified by a series of Institutional Acts issued by the military high command. The political party system was completely reorganized, and the electoral procedures and standards of the 1946 Republic were severely modified. Two new parties, ARENA (the National Renovating Alliance) and the MDB (Brazilian Democratic Movement), emerged as the two parties of the Military Republic. The ARENA attracted the bulk of the UDN and the conservative PSD members; the MDB, the opposition party, appealed to the PTB and left wing of the PSD and members of the leftist-leaning smaller parties.

A number of former politicians and public servants were declared ineligible for public office; many had their political rights removed for ten years. After direct gubernatorial elections were held in October 1965, and two candidates identified as opposed to the regime had won, the electoral laws were again rewritten to provide for the indirect election of state governors. The Second Institutional Act of October 1965 further centralized administrative and political power in the hands of the military president. In 1966 the minister of war in Castello Branco's cabinet, General Arthur da Costa e Silva, emerged as the military's candidate for the presidency.

Costa e Silva assumed office in March 1967 at the same time that a new constitution was promulgated after being rubber-stamped by the congress. The new government retained the broad policy outlines of its predecessor. The fight against inflation continued, with relative success. The congress was allowed a ceremonial role in policy-making, but even that was foreclosed with the congressional crisis of December 1968.

Refusing to remove the immunity of one of its members who stood accused of defaming the integrity of the armed forces, the government recessed the congress indefinitely. It did not meet again until March 1970. With the recession of Congress, President Costa e Silva governed by decree. The bureaucracy of the central government continued to make and implement policy with little need to be concerned with popular opinion or legislative monitoring.

With the incapacitation of the president in August, 1969, the Military Republic moved into its second phase, which continues today: one of increased authoritarianism. With the publication of a series of Institutional Acts and a Constitutional Amendment, the military further centralized political power in the central government and gave the military regime the means to dominate society totally. When it became clear that President Costa e Silva would not recover his health, the military commanders bypassed the civilian vice-president, Pedro Aleixo, an old UDN politician from Minas Gerais, declared the presidency vacant, and proceeded to select another army officer. Congress ratified the military selection, General Emílio Garrastazu Médici, on October 25, 1969. His term of office ends March 25, 1974.

Elections under the Military Republic have been passive events after the drama of the October 1965 incident. Careful screening of all candidates, indirect election of governors, and the appointment of the mayors of important cities by the state governors have all contributed to make the electoral system a sham. The ARENA has dominated all the elections held. The MDB, after the gubernatorial and congressional elections of 1970, has fallen into a distinctly subsidiary place.

As of 1972, the Military Republic appears well-established. The primary opposition groups — the Church, the students, and the urban terrorists — have been co-opted or defeated, as we shall see in chapter 5, in the traditional patrimonial style in which all governments have governed Brazil. The military no longer think of themselves as "caretakers" but as the legitimate successors of the corrupt 1946 Republic. They have assumed responsibility for the direction of the patrimonial state on the same terms that all previous regimes have done. Basic power alignments are left undisturbed, and the emphasis chosen by the regime — economic development — is pursued with the same disregard for public opinion and popular participation that Vargas showed in emphasizing social and economic reform during the Transitional Republic.

THE PATRIMONIAL REGIME

The interpretation of Brazilian political development set out in *Os Donos do Poder,* by Raymundo Faoro, emphasizes the power of the state in Brazilian society from the settlement period into the twentieth century. Faoro represents one of two dominant themes in analyzing the evolution of Brazilian politics; the other concentrates on the power of the local, rural aristocracy — on the pervading influence of the private sector in the creation and use of public power.[22] For our purposes, Faoro's interpretation is more realistic and relevant for contemporary Brazil.

Faoro stresses the role of the central government bureaucracy in managing the interventionist policies of the patrimonial regime. Unlimited by popular influence, the *patronato político*, or patronal political authority of the public sector, established the parameters within which the social and economic structures of Brazilian society evolved. State capitalism provided the major impetus for economic growth; the limited franchise and the elitist domination of public policy-making by the public functionaries, the clergy, the military, and the landowners assured a hierarchial social system that stratified society over time and between two groups: upper and lower.

The bureaucratic state has rarely, if ever, yielded its domination to the power of the majority — thus, "minority power," or the power of the few, has characterized Brazilian society from its founding (with due allowance for different actors in different historical periods). In periods when the concept of representative government has emerged in the political process, the constitution and the popularly elected delegates of the people have been a superficial cover for the continuing influence of the patrimonial regime.

Simon Schwartzman, building on Faoro's interpretation, identifies two different political systems emerging in Brazil over time.[23] One has been representative and "democratic" and appeared in the relatively developed Center-South region, primarily in and around the state of São Paulo. The other, a system of political co-optation, characterizes the Western and Northeastern states. As Brazil developed in the twentieth century, the two political systems coexisted uneasily; the most apparent period of rivalry between the two was during the

[22]Nestor Duarte, *A Ordem Privada e a Organização Política Nacional* (São Paulo: Companhia Editôra Nacional, 1939).

[23]Simon Schwartzman, "Representação a cooptação Política no Brasil," *Dados* (Rio de Janeiro), No. 7, pp. 9-41.

short-lived 1946 Republic. The 1946 Republic provided the framework within which the two systems — representative and co-optive — battled for supremacy. With the prolonged crisis of 1961-64 and the military coup of March 31, 1964, the limited representative system floundered and then collapsed.

The representative political system functioned only in the Center-South, and then only spasmodically, where the rate of urbanization and the level of literacy and social mobilization provided a sufficiently large and aware body politic. The system of political co-optation neatly complemented the patrimonial state. The non-issue orientation of campaigns and political debates in the 1946 Republic reflected the inability of candidates to stand for office on any basis other than their personal appeal and the personal loyalty and support of a segment of the electorate — that is, populist politics.

The failure of the representative and rational order to dominate politics reflected the ability and willingness of the bureaucratic state to buy off and neutralize any independent challenge or threat to its position. Through the use of patronage and public power, potential opponents were co-opted by the system, leaving a small number concentrated in the Center-South to lead the battle against the immobilism that characterized — and characterizes — the public order. Immune to reform and restructuring, the weight of the patrimonial state fell behind the armed forces in 1964 as they moved to protect Brazil from the threats of change and revolution that Goulart and his cohorts posed.

The patrimonial state represents the "minority power" of the few in Brazilian society. Most Brazilians, the "majority power" of the state, have never been involved in policy-making or governance. When the people have been allowed to elect their representatives freely, the latter have been successfully co-opted into the orbit of the patrimonial regime. São Paulo, where the patrimonial regime has weakened because of the economic preeminence of that state, has been systematically excluded from exercising public power commensurate with its social and economic stature in the republic; the premier role of Minas Gerais, Rio Grande do Sul, and one or two of the Northeastern states is due to their willingness to cooperate with the center in order to insure their social and political survival.

The concept of the patrimonial state works on two levels of importance for our understanding of Brazilian politics. The first is the practical level. Here successive regimes, and the governments of those regimes, structure and rule Brazil as the guardians of the power (coercive and noncoercive) of the state. In this sense, the state is often synonomous with the regime or the government. The latter, when exercising authority in relation to its subjects, *is* the state. The second level is one of abstraction. It is at this level that the state provides a general framework for political action by regimes and their governments. In so providing, the state appears as the embodiment of the historical and social processes that have most influenced the formation of the nation or the society. In this role the state is greater than the sum of its regimes over time. Once created, the state assumes a vitality and meaning of its own that is not easily amendable. The state provides the general parameters within which the society functions. Its political system must work within these confines or run the risk of losing its authority. For it is, in the last analysis, how faithful a regime is to the image of the state constructed through the centuries, and accepted by a majority of the population and especially the politically elite, that establishes its credibility or legitimacy.

In Brazil, the concept of the state is one of a predominance of public over private power. From the early years of colonization and settlement, the state intervened in all spheres of societal activity. The state assumed primary responsibility for economic and social development, which is often left to private sector initiative in other societies. The Brazilian state has been an interventionist state, a paternalistic state, an authoritarian state. It did not replicate the Western liberal and democratic model although the *institutions* of that model would later be implanted in Brazil, providing a confusing and misleading sense of change. Nor did it approximate a totalitarian state in which every facet of societal existence is closely regulated by the coercive power of the central authority.

The patrimonial state is perhaps best described as a residual state in terms of power application: through custom as well as usage its preeminence is accepted and safeguarded. To accomplish its purposes in Brazil, the state was — and is — willing to allow limited political activity as long as the actors adhere to the established rules. This provides for a flexible and resourceful system of control. It allows for diversity — social and economic — which is a dominant characteristic of Brazil. In exchange for political support from the dominant social factors in society, the patrimonial state confirms and supports their local socioeconomic hegemony.

The state in Brazil recognizes new and potentially disruptive social and political forces and acts to incorporate them into the prevailing order. The labor movement is perhaps the best example wherein the labor unions were organized and tied to the government long before mass popular demand for organizational independence appeared. Thus, a potential threat to the political equilibrium of the state was forestalled.

The concern of this type of state is its authority and the unfettered exercise of that authority. It possesses the capacity to control society coercively but prefers to utilize the techniques of persuasion, tradition, and co-option. While it is insistent on dominating, it is not insistent on regulating, and this is a decisive difference from totalitarian states. Regulation of many issues is left to local initiative with the understanding that local initiative, regardless of *its* diversity, will be supportive of the general system of power previously established.

What is to be stressed is that the state is not monolithic, nor is the national elite which manipulates its political system. The key characteristics, in addition to survival, are adaptability, resiliency, and omnipresence in every activity of the society. Working through and with the complicity of the political elite, the state penetrates and dominates the nation. But the consolidation and extension of its power is explicable in terms of its own interests, which may or may not coincide with the interests and the needs of the citizenry.

ELITES IN BRAZIL

Beginning with the colonial rule of Portugal and continuing today with the military regime of March 31, 1964, political power has been concentrated in the hands of a small, relatively homogeneous elite or leadership group.

The Brazilian elite can be divided into a "ruling class" and a "political elite," distinctions drawn from the literature on elites and society.[24] The power of a ruling class stems from its ownership of property. It is composed of a group of families which remains at its core from generation to generation. The most distinctive members of the ruling class in Brazil are the sugar plantation owners and cattle ranchers of the Northeast, the coffee entrepreneurs in São Paulo, and the cattle ranchers of Minas Gerais and Rio Grande do Sul.

The political elite's power is built on its influence with the institutions of the patrimonial state of which the bureaucracy, the Church, and the military are the most important. While there is a certain amount of social cohesion that characterizes the ruling class, this is not so of the political elite. The driving force behind the political elite is its desire for public power. The two groups have cooperated together effectively for generations; their goals have complemented each other. For the ruling class, the primary objective has been to prevent any reorganization of land tenure, the basis of its wealth and influence. It also opposes all efforts to organize the rural workers or to introduce into the rural zone the benefits of modern society. The political elite, concerned primarily with achieving public office and access to the patronage benefits of the public power, cares little about real reform. Its interests are in holding power, whether appointive or elective, and this has required the tacit support of the ruling class. In exchange for that support, no reforms that would disturb the hegemony of the ruling class in the rural areas have been considered seriously.

The military, recruited not from the ruling class primarily, are de facto members of the political elite because of their monopoly of the society's organized force. After 1946 the military became increasingly sympathetic with the social and political goals of the ruling class. The convergence of interests between the military and the ruling class centered on the fear of social and economic upheaval in the countryside. To one it represented a challenge to socioeconomic influence; to the other, a threat to internal security and a challenge to the

[24]T.B. Bottomore, *Elites and Society* (London: Penguin Books, 1967), especially chapter 2.

constitutional and historical role of the armed forces in Brazil. We shall use the term *national elite* to refer to both the ruling class and the political elite.

The Brazilian national elite has been little studied. All we can do is indicate in general terms its composition and main attributes. First and foremost, the elite is permeable, susceptible to infiltration by new members as long as the aspirants are willing to accept and defend the basic rules and prerogatives of the patrimonial state. (Thus, Presidents Getúlio Vargas and Juscelino Kubitschek were acceptable; Presidents Jânio Quadros and João Goulart were not.) These rules are, principally, to avoid the political mobilization of the masses, especially in the countryside; to maintain a ban against illiterates' voting (in support of the first objective); to leave untouched land tenure and land utilization patterns; to guarantee the continuation of sugar prices in the Northeast and coffee prices in the South; to limit the educational system to a minority of the population, having it serve mainly to ratify the principles of the patrimonial state and as a source of manpower for it; to smother any originality and proclivity for independence in the labor movement; to foster industrialization through import substitution; to subordinate overall economic development programs to the needs of national security. This listing is suggestive, not definitive; it seeks to provide, in general terms, the scheme of action of the Brazilian political system.

These are the objectives to which the national elite has been consistently loyal. Even regime changes have not altered (although personnel has changed) the commitment to a traditional and tutelary patrimonial state. The national elite in Brazil revolves around the chief executive and the military forces. Connected to the elite through the chief executive are appropriate state governors, the federal bureaucracy, and a limited number of regional political leaders who may or may not be members of parliament, and members of the hierarchy of the Roman Catholic Church.

The national elite is well served by a network of control and communications spread throughout the country. The major segments of this network are the four regional army commands (located in Rio de Janeiro [I Army], São Paulo [II Army], Porto Alegre [III ARMY], and Recife [IV Army] and the

Military Command of the Amazon in Manaus) and the subordinate garrisons in smaller cities; the all-pervasive central bureaucracy and governmental autarchies (especially in the Northeast); governors and members of parliament of peripheral states; and regional and local officials of the Roman Catholic Church.

The national elite is self-perpetuating. Its members serve less as individuals and more as representatives of the social and institutional interests from which they come. Thus, the minister of war is always a key figure in the elite, but his credibility is established not by the power of his own personality — although this may be a contributing factor — but primarily by his ability to uphold the interests of the military establishment within the framework of the prevailing system of power. (Thus, War Ministers Henrique Lott and Odílio Denys were successful in the 1950s and early 1960s; most of the war ministers of João Goulart were not.)

In the same way, the national elite tolerates personal dishonesty (Adhemar de Barros, mayor and governor of São Paulo and twice presidential candidate) if the individual accepts the rules of the game. It mercilessly undercuts and isolates men personally honest but perceived as threatening to the authoritarian state (Governor Miguel Arraes in Pernambuco, 1963-64, and economist Celso Furtado, Superintendent of the Northeast Development Agency, SUDENE, 1959-64). Personal integrity is less important than personal loyalty to the authoritarian state.

The national elite succeeds because it is united; it survives because it is flexible and adaptive; it serves the interests of the patrimonial state while it serves its own through unalterable but muted opposition to potentially disruptive systemic inputs such as "basic reforms" (João Goulart) and personal power exercised independently of the framework of the authoritarian state (Getúlio Vargas in 1945). Its subtle presence is often overlooked because it is so pervasive; its power becomes readily apparent when we examine the crises leading to changes in regime in Brazil.

Over time the national elite has co-opted and absorbed new members (in the 1950s and 1960s technocrats and planners, for example), and it has successfully eliminated contentious members or those who have deliberately broken the understood procedures for permissible criticism of the patrimonial system (Ruy Barbosa between 1900 and 1920; Dom Hélder Câmara, archbishop of Recife and Olinda since 1964; and former Governor Carlos Lacerda of Guanabara in the 1960s and early 1970s). It has survived serious crises, inter-regime (the 1930 Revolution and the 1945 Vargas deposition), and intra-regime (November 1955 attempted coup d'état to prevent President-elect Kubitschek's assuming power and the August-September 1961 military intervention to prevent Vice-President Goulart's succeeding Jânio Quadros). It has moved quickly and, on the whole, effectively, from its point of view, to incapacitate any political movement possessing potential for political mobilization or disruption (fascists and communists in the mid-1930s and the Peasant Leagues and Rural Labor Union Movement in the Northeast in the 1960s).

This is not a "conspiracy theory" explanation of political power. It is an attempt to cut through the meaningless rhetoric which surrounds the discussion of politics in Latin America and particularly Brazil. What is important here is to grasp the concept of elite control without serious opposition; elite domination without serious political dislocations within the political system.

INTEGRATION AND NATIONAL IDENTITY

Other variables important for our framework are those of integration and national identity. The national elite of the Brazilian patrimonial state has had little sustained interest in effectively integrating the majority of the population into a commonly held conception of the nation-state. The issue in Brazil has not been a crisis of identity, as it is in the new states and nations of Africa and Asia. Rather, it has been a deliberate objective of the political elite, operating through the patrimonial state, to ignore or deliberately preclude serious consideration of the question. Consequently, Brazil remains, in the late twentieth century, a nation-state ill prepared for a popular participatory form of government based upon the informed and mature involvement of the majority of its citizens.

The level of psychological membership of the average

Brazilian citizen in the nation-state remains abysmally low. The exception would be residents of the few major metropolitan areas and those groups, such as students and labor leaders, who have been politicized over time. While, to the average Brazilian, "Brazil" has symbolic value, in that it is real in a legal and geographical sense, his feeling of participation and involvement is shallow. He has had few opportunities to participate directly in national affairs; the citizen remains geographically isolated in his region, psychologically incapable of identifying his immediate needs and interests with those of a national society.

Save for a brief period during the presidency of João Goulart (1961-64) — and then in a disorganized and bombastic fashion — the national elite has chosen to ignore the issues of integration and national identity in Brazil. Under the Military Republic there has been a growing concern for renewing the process of territorial integration in the Amazon basin for reasons of both economic development and national security. A recurrence in 1970 of the episodic droughts that afflict the Northeast region led to a renewal of government discussion about the need to seek more drastic remedies for dealing with the economic backwardness of that area. These are exceptions to the general rule that the issue of integration is not one for general discussion and debate.

There are three aspects of the general issue of integration that require some examination. These are value integration, elite-mass integration, and the development of integrative behavior in the society. These are subdivisions of the overall integration problem, that of trying to define what it is "which holds a society and a political system together."[25] Let us examine each of these briefly.

Value integration refers to the existence, at a minimum, of "acceptable procedures for the resolution of conflict." All societies have conflicts, and all possess some procedures for their resolution. But the procedures are not always satisfactory in that they are not acceptable to a sufficiently large or important segment of the society. There will be a breakdown of public order and potential or actual conflict unless agreement

[25]Myron Weiner, "Political Integration and Political Development," *The Annals,* Vol. 358 (March, 1965), 52-64.

can be reached among those participating in public life as to the measures to be employed in resolving differences. In Brazil, where value integration is low, the military have been the traditional intervener in the political process to forestall civilian conflict. But military intervention has not led to an attempt at creating integrative values in Brazil — merely to the avoidance of bloodshed. The issue has been shunted aside in favor of an elite solution to the problem.

Elite-mass integration refers to the establishment of a pattern of authority and consent between governed and governors; it does not require the disappearance of differences between the two, but it would seem to indicate that both participate in the quest for meaningful patterns of communication and information exchange in order to provide the governors with the information they require to govern and to provide the governed with a feeling of participation in their society.

Integrative behavior indicates "the readiness of individuals to work together in an organized fashion for common purposes and to behave in a fashion conducive to the achievement of these common purposes in an essential behavioral pattern of complex modern societies."[26] The assumption underlying this proposition is that a modicum of sustained participation by the mass is required for the full development of the physical and human resources of the society.

What holds Brazilian society and its political system together are, of course, the patrimonial state and its national elite. Any discussion of integration and the need for increased national identity is perceived by the elite as a possible challenge to their position. They interpret the country's future in terms of their own goals. The needs of Brazil are satisfied within the framework we have been discussing in this chapter. Further expansion of the elite or any deliberate program to educate and integrate the masses politically would lead to instability, and instability in any form is deleterious to the elite's continuation in power.

Integrative behavior has not developed in Brazil because it is so often identified with partisan and parochial political goals

[26]Ibid.

that threaten to destabilize the regime. Value integration and elite-mass integration are direct challenges to the elitist, exclusive interpretation of society which prevails in Brazil today.

The vast majority of Brazil's citizens remain, in Almond and Verba's terminology, political *subjects*.[27] That minority classifiable as political *participants* identifies the national political elite and their regional and state counterparts and dependents. The issues of identity and integration in Brazil are issues that the political elite wish to avoid. It is a peculiar characteristic of Brazilian history that changes in regime, to say nothing of government changes within regimes, have occurred with little or no popular participation. Major issues such as economic development in general or industrialization and nationalization of economic resources have remained elite issues. After 1946 a split in the political elite led to the manipulation of the mass citizenry, principally in the urban areas, by politicians identified as populists. Renegade members of the political elite as well as disenchanted members of regional elites, they sought mass support to challenge the patrimonial state. The confrontation years of 1961 to 1964 ended with their defeat and the direct assumption of power by the military who have always played a crucial role within the national elite. It should be noted that most of the populist leaders of this period seemed to evidence no greater interest in meaningful mass involvement on a continuing basis than had their erstwhile "conservative" opponents.

The lack of national identity — the poorly developed sense of national integration, in political terms — helps explain the continuing success of the national elite and the domination of the state. The highest level of political awareness that the majority of citizens possess, save in a symbolic sense, is the local community or perhaps the state. This has left the regional concept a viable one in Brazilian politics. Local and regional

[27]Gabriel A. Almond and Sidney Verba, *The Civic Culture* (Boston and Toronto: Little, Brown and Company, 1963).

The author's threefold classification is parochial: subject-participant, representing the transition from unawareness of politics, to being a "consumer" of political goods but not a "contributor" to the system, to, finally, full participatory status in the political system.

political leaders are able in times of "open" politics, when restricted national suffrage is allowed (1946 Republic), to deliver the votes required to maintain the patrimonial state. In times of "closed" politics, when the suffrage is meaningless or nonexistent (the Transitional Republic, the *Estado Novo,* the Military Republic), there is little, if any, popular protest against what is accepted as a "national" state of affairs. This has provided extraordinary opportunities for flexibility for the political elite to determine its own program and work to fulfill its goals without fear of popular pressure. Only at those times of crisis when the national elite has splintered has there been a change of regime in Brazil. Each change of regime has manifested minimal political participation by the masses, confirming the highly specialized nature of the elite and demonstrating one of its primary operating rules (broken in the 1961 to 1964 period which required armed military intervention), which is that changes in the composition of elite are intra-elite. In this way the state has both prospered and dominated Brazilian political life since the discovery of the country in 1500.

IMPLICATIONS OF THE POLITICAL "GIVENS" IN BRAZIL

It is a general thesis of this book that Brazilian politics can best be understood in terms of a powerful, patrimonial state directed by a national political elite. Federalism has been the form of organization adopted to meet the political and administrative needs of the state and not the needs of the provinces or states. Regionalism has been and remains a potent factor in political life because the internal dynamics of the authoritarian state revolve around the economic and political rivalries and alliances of the nation's five regions, particularly the Northeast, the Southeast, and the South.

Given the low level of national political integration and identity among Brazilians, the more parochial and particularistic level of the region or state remains the relevant reference for public affairs. The political elite, regardless of its momentary objectives — to attract foreign investment, to protect coffee prices, or to foster import substitution and industrialization — feels little need to seek popular support for its program. The policy of the patrimonial state to identify its goals without consultation with the people and to act independently of any expressed opinion of the people is a long-standing and venerable tradition in Brazil. This tradition, combined with little, if any, sustained political mobilization of a majority of the population, provides an uncomplicated and relatively efficient means for the political elite both to survive and to govern the nation.

Given the almost meaningless content of the federal democratic state in Brazil, elections and political representation are, by and large, what the political elite says that they are. The continuing importance of the regions is understandable in terms of the desire of the elite to maintain, for both traditional-historical and pragmatic-political reasons, the near-fiction of a functioning federal system. In reality it is the region and not the federation which is most relevant politically. The power concentrated in the state is dispersed regionally (and then only to the most powerful states who serve as regional power centers) and not federally. The federation functions, intermittently, when and only when the state desires it and then only through the political directives sent to the regional political elites from the center.

Thus, state executives — whether they are titled presidents (Old Republic), interventors (Transitional Republic), or governors (1946 and Military Republics) — are figures of influence only if they have appropriate ties to the center and are so recognized by the national elite. Often they serve as mere delegates to the periphery of the political system on behalf of the center. Their participation in national politics, if they are from one of the five or six major states, is certain; their success in politics is determined by circumstances other than their federal role as the governor or executive of a state. What is important is their role in their region and the implications this has for the program of the national elite. Thus, while it is governors who play a prominent role in national politics in Brazil (unlike the United States, where senators have come to dominate the national scene) to the detriment of their congressional colleagues, that role is functional only when they are willing to operate on terms previously set out by the national elite. Membership in that elite is relatively easy for a governor willing and able to play his assigned role; but in exchange he loses a great deal of the autonomy his position should provide him. The issue is relatively simple: autonomy without linkage to the center and little real power, or linkage to the center and participation in national power without autonomy. It is not surprising that most governors have opted for the latter. The case of Jânio Quadros is, of course, instructive. A former state governor who sought to control the center and maintain his autonomy, he survived but eight months (January-August 1961) as president of the republic.

If the position of the state executives is somewhat weaker vis-à-vis the patrimonial state, the federal congress (both the chamber of deputies and the senate) is even more marginal. While the state always requires regional and state delegates — the governors — for both administrative and political purposes, the congress is expendable. It functions when the interests of the state require the "normal" functioning of the federal, democratic state. When it does not, the congress is closed, and the state, of course, continues to function.

The two most dramatic examples of the downgrading of the federal congress are those of the Transitional Republic and the Military Republic. During both of these eras the congress has been unceremoniously closed to meet the immediate needs of the patrimonial state. The justification normally has been that its continuation would be "disruptive" to the program of the government. During the Old Republic there was little need to close the congress formally; it docilely performed the limited functions assigned to it by the national elite. Its role was prestigious in that membership in it was granted via a limited, circumscribed electoral system to a variety of state and regional political figures.

The explanation for the marginality of the congress is simple. In a functioning federal system it is the legislative branch of the government that poses the greatest check and balance to the prerogatives of the executive. In the Brazilian federal system, the congress serves less a legislative function and more of either a brake on executive "progressivism" (the 1946 Republic particularly from 1961 to 1964) or a formal "ratifier" of national elite decision-making exercised through the chief executive on behalf of the authoritarian state.

The "need" for the congress is quite formal and historical. When Brazil adopted a federative form of organization borrowed from the Western states, a legislature was a necessity. In addition, it served a utilitarian purpose in working out the political relationship between the center and the regions and states in that it could be used to reward faithful retainers. It also served as an anteroom for those about to be absorbed into the central power structure, or as a safety valve for those few recalcitrants who refused to cooperate with the national elite and who possessed sufficient local or regional support to require making room at the top.

3
Political Parties and Elections

Of all the major political systems in Latin America, political parties have probably played the smallest role in the development of the Brazilian system. Mexico's PRI, the Radicals in Argentina and Chile, APRA in Peru, and the Conservatives and Liberals in Colombia are all examples of parties having a relatively long period of growth and impact on the national political system. In contrast, Brazilian parties have too closely resembled "the small oligarchial groups which take the name of party" but in reality "are more akin to the factions of notables in the Roman Republic."[1] Parties in Brazil have been subservient to the "givens" we have identified in the political process. They have played a marginal role in exercising decision-making power; they have demonstrated little continuity in organization at the national or local level; and they have evidenced only minimal interest in seeking popular support for reasons other than immediate electoral goals. The party system has not been viewed as a legitimate means of resolving disputes in Brazil in any phase of national development. It has done little to further national integration or to reduce and resolve political cleavages. In fact, parties in Brazil, particularly in the 1946 Republic, exacerbated social and political conflicts rather than helping to "manage" them. They have not been a means of

[1] Joseph La Palombara and Myron Weiner, *Political Parties and Political Development* (Princeton: Princeton University Press, 1966), p. 7.

socializing people into the political system, nor have they been able to fulfill vital input functions in the political system: articulating and aggregating interests. Parties have not been legitimized in the eyes of the citizens of Brazil.

The following historical sketch provides a setting for considering parties during the 1946 Republic, the only period of open, competitive party politics in Brazilian history. An analysis of Brazilian parties is instructive because it demonstrates the impact of the patrimonial regime on all aspects of political life and enables us to trace the development and decay of the 1946 Republic. The party system of that period, when contrasted with the Military Republic, will give us an enhanced view of politics in Brazil.

PARTIES UNTIL 1946

During the Empire (1822-89) the Liberal and Conservative Parties were divided less by policy differences and more by individual and regional rivalries and loyalties. The Liberals, formed in 1831, and the Conservatives, organized in 1837, were rotated in power at the whim of the emperor. The predominant political figures of the Empire were not known as "party men" but as individuals who rendered exceptional and loyal service to the monarch.

Save for the short-lived Progressive Party, formed in the 1860s by the left wings of the two parties, the only new attempt at organized political activity was the Republican Party, created in 1870. The Manifesto of 1870, the founding document of the party, advocated well-known reform measures previously proposed by the Liberal Party. The first state Republican organization was that formed in São Paulo in 1873. Not until 1885 did the party succeed in electing its first candidates to Parliament. While the party supported abolition of slavery, it did not do so fervently; while the Republicans favored reform, they did not endorse radical change; and while they favored a republic, most of their number were wealthy, comfortable conservatives. It can be said that the Brazilian republican movement gained adherents in spite of, and not because of, the Republican Party.

With the creation of the Old Republic (1889-1930) under military aegis, the Liberal and the Conservative Parties disintegrated. The state Republican Party units became the political nucleus of the Old Republic. The patrimonial regime from 1889 to 1930 utilized the Republican Party to run the country with the cooperation of its regional and state units; the latter normally functioned only at election time. Only twice did the Republican Party not succeed in imposing its official candidates on the country. In 1910, Marshal Hermes da Fonseca, with military and partial party endorsement, gained the presidency. In 1918, with a split in the political elite, Epitácio Pessoa was chosen to succeed a president who had died in office. Opposition candidates had little, if any, chance of victory given the careful understanding between state and federal governments. Only in 1910 and 1914 did an opposition candidate, without an organized party organization, stand against the establishment. In both elections Rui Barbosa, a statesman of the Empire, was defeated.

One of the few attempts to organize an opposition to the Republican Party was the Democratic Party of São Paulo. Formed in 1926 by middle-class urban groups in the city of São Paulo, the party had little success in challenging the political elite. The Democratic Party supported the candidacy of Vargas in 1930. Participation in elections was limited for a number of reasons. In a predominantly rural and agrarian nation, the constitutional restriction against illiterates voting excluded the vast majority of the potential electorate. Regional and state political and social controls, exercised by the elites, precluded deviant or active political activity by literate citizens. Thus, in the election of 1910, in which there was competition for president, only 1.64 percent of the total population voted. In 1914, 2.14 percent voted; and, in 1930, the only other election year during the Old Republic with more than one presidential candidate, 5.10 percent of the total population cast their ballot. In terms of numbers of votes, Júlio Prestes in 1930 was the first presidential candidate to receive more than one million votes. He defeated Getúlio Vargas but lost the presidency with the Revolution of 1930.

From the successful revolution in October 1930 to the promulgation of the 1934 constitution, the political party scene remained fluid. The Republican Party and the Democratic Party in São Paulo joined forces; both groups feared that Vargas and his entourage were determined to break the national political influence of that state. The friction over Vargas's interveners, economic policy, and the future place of the state in national affairs led to the revolt of July 9, 1932. The other states of the federation did not come to São Paulo's assistance, and the rebels surrendered on September 29, 1932.

The Partido de Lavoura, organized by Vargas's intervener in São Paulo, never received widespread support. It slowly withered away, and with the revolt of 1932 it disappeared for all practical purposes.

The national political party system remained confused until 1934. In some states the old Republican Party merged with new groups; in other states the Republican Party disintegrated and was replaced by an amorphous organization that represented the immediate interests of those whom the revolutionary government recognized and had appointed to positions of influence; and in São Paulo and Minas Gerais, the Republican Party maintained its autonomy.

The young *tenentes,* who had helped bring Vargas to power, organized a number of clubs, none of which was sufficiently structured and coherent to be mistaken for a political party. The 5th of October Club, the date of the successful 1930 Revolution, was the best known. Others were the 5th of July Club and the Agrarian Party. All these organizational attempts were in support of the vague and idealistic reform program the *tenentes* hoped to see implemented after Vargas assumed power. By 1932-33, the *tenentes* had fragmented; their program had been co-opted by the regime or sidetracked by other concerns.

The election in May 1933 for a constituent assembly to write a new constitution was confused from the political party perspective. The ballots of the states included hundreds of parties and organizations, none of which were national, and few, if any, of which had a mass following. With the proclamation of the 1934 constitution, two new political movements came into prominence and the old parties declined in influence.

The Integralists (Brazilian Integralist Association — AIB)

and the Communists became the dominant political movements from 1934 to 1937. Both were the first ideologically based parties in Brazil. *Integralismo* had come into existence in October 1932 with a "Manifesto to the Brazilian Nation" by their leader, a writer from São Paulo, Plínio Salgado. Influenced by the dictatorships of Europe, particularly Mussolini in Italy and Salazar in Portugal, the movement was conservative, nationalist, traditionalist and Roman Catholic in orientation.

The Communist Party, led by Luís Carlos Prestes, a former *tenente,* continued to grow in popular appeal after 1930. Its leader had been a well-known opposition figure during the Old Republic. The appeal of the party to the masses captured the imagination of segments of the Brazilian population as the first signs of an urban proletariat emerged. In 1935 the National Liberating Alliance (ANL) was created with Prestes as honorary president. Publicized as a popular-front type of organization, it was clear that the Communist Party was the principal member and instigator of its activities.

Vargas maintained formal and informal contacts with Plínio Salgado and Luís Carlos Prestes throughout the early and mid-1930s.[2] As the old political parties seemed unable to claim widespread popular support, Vargas saw the two opposing movements as possible alternatives for support for his program. Vargas played the one against the other; they were allowed to organize freely. The clashes between the two groups increased during 1934 and 1935. Bloody street fighting erupted in the major cities. The growing tension culminated with communist uprisings in the Northeast, in Pernambuco, and Rio Grande do Norte; in November 1935 a raid on a federal military garrison in Rio de Janeiro resulted in a number of officers being murdered. The uprising was put down by the government, the party outlawed, and Prestes jailed.

The suppression of the communists coincided with the growing tension surrounding the presidential election of 1937; Vargas's term of office, under the 1934 constitution, ended in 1938. Two candidates emerged: former *tenente* José Américo de Almeida, the government candidate, and the governor of São Paulo, Armando Sales, who spoke for the anti-regime forces.

[2] For an excellent analysis of this period, see Robert M. Levine, *The Vargas Regime* (New York and London: Columbia University Press, 1970).

The campaign progressed bitterly. The nation seemed hopelessly polarized. Rumors of a government coup began to circulate.

Vaguely promising a preferred position for the Integralists in the political order if they supported his coup, Vargas, on November 10, 1937, decreed the New State.

On December 3, 1937, the president dissolved all political parties. Not even the Integralists were allowed to survive organizationally. Slowly Vargas had outwitted or defeated all organized political opposition. The old Republican units had been discredited or relegated to a marginal position in national politics; the feeble organizational efforts of the *tenentes* and their idealistic supporters had been allowed to wither; the few semiorganized opposition parties of the Old Republic, such as the Democratic Party of São Paulo, were found wanting and allowed to decay; and the communists and Integralists, used and manipulated by Vargas, were dealt swift, effective blows when they no longer served the needs of the patrimonial state. In May 1938 the last gasp of the Integralists was a failure: an attempt to invade the presidential palace in Rio and murder the president.

Vargas's tactics undermined and destroyed the political party organizations of the 1930-37 period. No parties were allowed to function between 1937 and 1945. The patrimonial regime, presided over by Vargas, assumed all responsibility for decision-making.

THE 1946 REPUBLIC

With the abrupt overthrow of Vargas, the Brazilian political system encountered a mass electorate for the first time. The 1946 Republic paid more than lip service to the principles of liberal democracy which had been superficially adhered to in previous regimes. But the long tradition of the patrimonial state had not provided the institutions and mechanisms that a mass electorate required. Brazil, from 1946 to 1964, became a "praetorian society" in Samuel Huntington's conceptualization of political development.[3] That is, the political system mani-

[3] Samuel P. Huntington, *Political Order in Changing Societies* (New Haven and London: Yale University Press, 1968).

fested low levels of institutionalization and relatively high levels of participation.

Prior to 1945 the only institutions that had real value in terms of political power were those of the patrimonial state — the executive and the bureaucracy and those administrative agencies of the state that served to structure the central government's relations with its subordinate units. Suddenly other institutions and procedures, such as political parties and interest groups, were allowed to act autonomously. As they attempted to fulfill their defined roles in an open, competitive political system, they ran into the intractability of the patrimonial state.

The prolonged constitutional crisis of the 1961-64 period was the inevitable outcome of the clash between the operating political realities of Brazilian society and the imagined political changes that the 1946 Constitution represented. Once it became clear to those groups aligned to the patrimonial regime and the status quo — the bureaucrats, administrators, landowners, and urban middle class — that the challenge posed by the newly mobilized groups might succeed in breaking the power of the patrimonial state and give real meaning to the ideals of the 1946 Constitution, the military acted on behalf of the establishment and overthrew Goulart, thus restoring "order" to public affairs in Brazil.

Throughout the 1946 Republic the parties remained loose coalitions of state and local units.[4] Little discipline existed within the party structures. An individual or a small group tended to dominate party policy-making. Little attempt was made to create a mass base, particularly in the rural areas. Beset by personalism, unable to carve out a constructive role in the decision-making process, subject to the patronage largesse of the state, the parties soon became a group of competing cabals without long-range goals or ideological purpose. The parties confused the electorate as much as they represented and guided them. As one party failed to fulfill its campaign promises, the frustrated voters would turn to another party and then another.

[4] For an evaluation of this period that analyzes the role of parties, see Octavio Ianni et al, *Política e Revolução Social no Brasil* (Rio de Janeiro: Editôra Civilização Brasileira, 1965) and Fernando Pedreira, Março 31, *Civis e Militares no Precesso da Crise Brasileira* (Rio de Janeiro: José Alvaro Editor, 1964).

When the parties appeared bankrupt, electoral alliances emerged in the competition for votes.

Out of this confusing and hopeless welter of organizations and individuals there emerged a melange of political brokers or go-betweens who played an important role in the politics of the era. Their job was to make the populist political system function by rounding up the votes required by the bosses or candidates by whom they were retained. The classic figure of the *coronel,* the wealthy and prestigious landowner of the interior, gained new importance as he delivered the votes of his employees and dependents to the party that had arranged to buy them. The *cabo eleitoral,* or election chief, arranged for a few hundred or a few thousand votes in exchange for patronage or cash. His interest in his following was based on his need for their votes and, in turn, their need to have someone intercede with the bureaucratic state for favors.

The *coronel* and the *cabo eleitoral* were accompanied by the political phenomena such as the *cabide de emprêgo* (employment hanger), *panelinha* (little saucepan), and *igrejinha* (little church), all identified by Anthony Leeds in his study of Brazilian society. The *cabide* represents the phenomenon of multiple job holding in Brazil. The *panelinha* is "a relatively closed, completely informal primary group, held together in common interest by personal ties and including a roster of all key socio-politico-economic positions."[5] Typically, a *panelinha* might consist of a customs official, one or two lawyers, a well-placed businessman, an accountant, a banker, and an assortment of local, state, and federal officials — appointed and elected. Each would lend his expertise and range of contacts to the group, and in exchange his interests would be protected and advanced.

The *igrejinha* is somewhat more hierarchical than a *panelinha,* which is a collaborative effort of equals. There is normally a dominant figure in the *igrejinha* who promotes and protects the careers of his followers; in return, they supply him with information, support, and a wide range of contacts who can "get things done." These linkage phenomena played a vital

[5] Anthony Leeds, "Brazilian Careers and Social Structure: A Case History and Model," *American Anthropologist,* Vol. 66 (1964), 1321-47.

role in the disjointed politics of the 1946-64 period. To survive and prosper politically, an individual required informal, transitory alliances with like-minded citizens. The personalism and informality of politics is well illustrated by these relationships that had more meaning than formal parties or interest groups in furthering careers.

LOCAL POLITICS
IN THE 1946 REPUBLIC

The personalism that pervaded the political party structure of the 1946 Republic is well illustrated by local and state politics from 1946 to 1964. While political populism dominated the electoral politics of the urban areas, demonstrating the basic weakness of the party system as a mechanism for aggregating and articulating demands, the party system in rural areas was dominated by a more traditional, paternalistic figure: the local *coronel* (literally, colonel, a title given to the landed gentry during the Old Republic for membership in the National Guard).

The *coronel's* purpose was to gain favors from the state or federal government in exchange for the votes of those dependent on him in the areas of the interior he dominated. The *coronel* would often head a network of *cabos eleitorais* (election bosses), who would deliver their votes to him in exchange for cash or services.

The source of the *coronel's* power rested with the agricultural and politically parochial culture of the Brazilian rural regions. A few families of influence dominated all aspects of society; high levels of illiteracy, a social tradition of dependence on the local power figure, and economic control of the zone's employment insured that the few would dominate the majority. The *coronel* served as the intermediary between the highly structured, dependent communities and the emerging urban areas. Writing in 1961, Frank Bonilla described the situation in the following way:

The traditional situation in the rural and interior *munícipios* (municipalities) has been for power to lie in the hands of a few strong families. Since the emergence of national parties at the end of the Vargas dictatorship (1945) the family power blocs have generally associated themselves with one of the major parties, usually either the PSD or the UDN. These two groups, which are much alike in social composition, represented initially a split in the traditional ruling elite into pro-Vargas and anti-Vargas forces. The PSD is the political machine extending into the rural *municípios* that is the counterpart of the PTB, the urban-based popular voting force also organized under Vargas.[6]

Marvin Harris captured the substance of local politics when he wrote that "patronage is the binding force in party structure. The local chefes promise votes for the state bosses; the state bosses promise assistance in all matters requiring mediation between the county and the state." [7]

The classic study of the role and function of the *coronel* remains that of Victor Nunes Leal.[8] Other studies have described in detail the process of rounding up the vote on election day;[9] the control of a state's politics by four men over a forty-year period;[10] and the colorful and powerful lifestyle of four colonels of the interior of Pernambuco.[11]

In an analysis of party politics and elections in Brazil from 1946 to 1964, Glaucio Ary Dillon Soares demonstrated that "the conservative parties have a much stronger position in the Northeast, where they account for almost 70 percent of all representatives elected for the Congress, whereas in the Southeast they account for only 45 percent."[12] He concludes that while party politics in the South had become more ideological and class oriented, "politics in the Northeast is the politics of

[6] Frank Bonilla, "Rural Reform in Brazil," *American Universities Field Staff Reports*, Vol. 8, No. 4 (October, 1961), East Coast South America Series (Brazil).

[7] Marvin Harris, *Town and Country in Brazil* (New York: Columbia University Press, 1956), pp. 191-92.

[8] Victor Nunes Leal, *Coronelismo, Enxada e Voto: O município e o Regime Representativo no Brasil* (Rio de Janeiro: Editôra Forense, 1948).

[9] Jean Blondel, *As Condições da Vida Política no Estado da Paraíba,* translated from the French by Alcantara Nogueira (Rio de Janeiro: Fundação Getúlio Vargas, 1957).

[10] Marcus Odilon Ribeiro Coutinho, *Poder, Alegria dos Homens* (João Pessoa, Pb.: Gráfica "A Imprensa," 1965).

[11] Marcos Vinicius Vilaça and Roberto C. de Albuquerque, *Coronel, Coroneis* (Rio de Janeiro: Edições Tempo Brasileiro, 1965).

[12] Glaucio Ary Dillon Soares, "The Politics of Uneven Development: The Case of Brazil," in Seymour M. Lipset and Stein Rokkan (eds.), *Party Systems and Voter Alignments: Cross-National Perspectives* (New York: The Free Press, 1967), p. 477.

backwardness — the politics of tradition." [13]

Although the party system of the 1946 Republic was dissolved in 1965 by the military, the old parties continue to be primary structural units of Brazilian politics. Newspapers continue to refer to men in public life by their pre-1965 party label; political coalitions and feuds are defined in terms of the pre-1965 party system. Because the post-1965 parties, ARENA and the MDB, have failed to "take root," the civilian political life of the Military Republic, limited as it is, is best explicated in terms of the personalities, rivalries, and organizational characteristics of the 1946-64 parties.

THE MAJOR PARTIES
— THE "BIG THREE"

Getúlio Vargas organized two parties in 1945 in preparation for his postwar political role in Brazilian politics. The Social Democratic Party (PSD) came about through the efforts of the New State Interventors in the states. Many of the Old Republic political bosses at the local level, still alive and active, became PSD stalwarts. It attracted the bureaucrats, landowners, bankers, and industrialists who benefited from the state-directed economic program of Vargas and that of PSD presidents during the 1946 Republic.

The PSD elected Vargas's minister of war, General Dutra, in 1945 and Juscelino Kubitschek, former governor of Minas Gerais, in 1955. It supported Vargas after his reelection on the PTB ticket in 1950. The PSD collaborated with the Goulart administration from 1961 to 1964. The only period during the 1946 Republic when the PSD was "out of favor" was during the brief Quadros incumbency in 1961. (See Table 8 for data on presidential elections.) It dominated the national congress and state legislatures. Of all the postwar parties it had the strongest organizational base in the states and regions. Moderately conservative, although nonideological, the PSD favored a centralization of power, state participation in economic devel-

[13]Ibid., p. 490.

Table 8

VOTES AND PERCENTAGES OF VOTE OBTAINED BY MAJOR PARTIES IN
FOUR PRESIDENTIAL ELECTIONS: 1945, 1950, 1955, and 1960

Date	Candidate & Party	Vote	% of Vote
1945	Eurico Dutra	3,251,507	52.4
	Social Democratic Party		
	Eduardo Gomes	2,039,341	32.9
	Democratic National Party		
	Yeddo Fiuza	569,818	9.2
	Communist Party of Brazil		
	Rollim Telles	10,001	0.2
	Null Vote	329,338	5.3
	Total	6,200,005	100.0
1950	Getúlio Vargas	3,849,040	46.6
	Brazilian Labor Party		
	Eduardo Gomes	2,342,384	28.4
	Democratic National Party		
	Cristiano Machado	1,697,193	20.6
	Social Democratic Party		
	João Mangabeira	9,466	0.1
	Brazilian Socialist Party		
	Null Vote	356,906	4.3
	Total	8,254,989	100.0
1955	Juscelino Kubitschek	3,077,411	33.8
	Social Democratic Party		
	Juárez Távora	2,610,462	28.7
	Democratic National Party		
	Adhemar de Barros	2,222,725	24.4
	Social Progress Party		
	Plínio Salgado	714,379	7.9
	Popular Representation Party		
	Null Vote	472,037	5.2
	Total	9,097,014	100.0
1960	Jânio Quadros	5,636,623	44.8
	Democratic National Party		
	Henrique Lott	3,846,825	30.6
	Social Democratic Party		
	Brazilian Labor Party		
	Adhemar de Barros	2,195,709	17.4
	Social Progress Party		
	Null Vote	907,197	7.2
	Total	12,586,354	100.0

Source: Brazil: Election Factbook, No. 2, September 1965 (Washington, D.C.: Institute for the Comparative Study of Political Systems), pp. 56-57.

opment, and the continuation and elaboration of the Vargas welfare system. Throughout the 1946 Republic it represented *par excellence* the amorphous party of the patrimonial state: pliant, adaptive, nonreformist, and uninterested in social or political mobilization. For many years the president of the party was Amaral Peixoto, Vargas's son-in-law.

The second party Vargas created, and the "partner" of the PSD throughout the post-1946 era, was the Brazilian Labor Party (PTB). Its purpose was to capitalize on Vargas's following among the urban masses and organized labor. Vargas utilized the PTB to return to power in 1950. Predominantly urban in orientation, the PTB was most susceptible to communist influence in the 1946 Republic. It had strong rural support in the states of Amazonas and Rio Grande do Sul. Its platform was one of active nationalism, state intervention in the economy, and extended welfare benefits for the working class. The PTB was the most heterogeneous of the major parties. It attracted wealthy landowners like João Goulart, middle-level government employees, artisans, members of the new urban upper class who hoped to use the party for their advantage, and leftist intellectuals. Goulart, as minister of labor under Vargas and the successor to Vargas as party leader, attempted to use the party to control organized labor for the government's advantage. But only a minority of organized labor actively backed the party, and there was widespread resentment over government controls of the workers' movement and the paternalistic and corrupt policies of the labor ministry.[14]

The PTB was the junior member of the PSD-PTB coalition until 1961, when Goulart succeeded Quadros as president. With the rapid urbanization of Brazil after 1946, the party grew quickly in popularity. (See Table 9 for a comparison of party strength in the Congress.) The 1962 state and congressional elections indicated a growing electoral challenge by the PTB to the leadership of the PSD. By 1963 defections from other parties had made it the largest party in the chamber of deputies. The left wing of the party, represented by men like Leonel Brizola, Goulart's brother-in-law and former governor of Rio Grande do Sul, pushed for greater independence from the centerist-PSD position that Goulart occupied and advocated

[14]Octavio Ianni analyzes this period in *O Colapso do Populismo no Brasil* (Rio de Janeiro: Editôra Civilização Brasileira, 1968).

Table 9
PARTY REPRESENTATION IN THE BRAZILIAN FEDERAL CHAMBER
(BY NUMBER OF SEATS)

Party	1948	1950	1954	1958	1962
PSD — Social Democratic Party (*Partido Social Democrático*)	151	112	114	115	122
UDN — National Democratic Union (*União Democrático Nacional*)	77	81	74	70	94
PTB — Brazilian Labor Party (*Partido Trabalhista Brasileiro*)	22	51	56	66	109
PSP — Social Progressive Party (*Partido Social Progressista*)	4	24	32	25	22
PR — Republican Party (*Partido Republicano*)	7	11	19	17	5
PDC — Christian Democratic Party (*Partido Democrata Cristão*)	2	2	2	7	20
PTN — National Labor Party (*Partido Trabalhista Nacional*)	0	5	6	7	11
PST — Social Labor Party (*Partido Social Trabalhista*)	0	9	2	2	8
PL — Liberation Party (*Partido Libertador*)	1	5	8	3	3
PRP — Popular Representation Party (*Partido de Representação*)	2	2	3	3	4
PSB — Brazilian Socialist Party (*Partido Socialista Brasileiro*)	0	1	3	9	4
PRT — Republican Labor Party (*Partido Republicano Trabalhista*)	0	1	1	2	3
MTR — Labor Reform Movement (*Movimento Trabalhista Renovador*)	0	0	0	0	4
PCB — Brazilian Communist Party (*Partido Comunista Brasileira*)	14				
Without party or coalition	6	0	6	0	0
Total seats	286	304	326	326	409

Source: U.S. Army, *Area Handbook for Brazil* (1964), p. 314.

radical reform in economic and social areas. In the federal senate, the PTB stood second, with eighteen of sixty-six seats (three per state) in 1963; the PSD was first with twenty-one and the UDN third with fifteen.

The third major political party of the 1946 Republic, the National Democratic Union (UDN), attracted the anti-Vargas forces in 1945. Except for the victory of Quadros in 1960, whom the party had endorsed, it was the principal opposition party from 1946 to 1964. Without access to the vast patronage and financial support of the federal government, it survived by keeping alive the antipathy of its members to the political populism of Vargas and his heirs. With the 1964 coup d'état, the UDN became the "government party" in that its principal leaders staffed many of the cabinet posts of the military regime. A moderate, conservative party, it drew heavily on the liberal professions and intellectuals of the urban areas. Emphasizing individual and democratic liberties, decentralized government, and honesty and efficiency in government, it remained a basically middle-class party. Men such as Carlos Lacerda, former governor of Guanabara, gave the party its reputation as an implacable enemy of the PSD-PTB governments. During the Quadros administration, the *Bossa Nova* (New Look) left wing of the party backed the president's independent foreign and domestic policies.

With the elections of 1958 and 1962, UDN governors were elected in many states for the first time. Magalhães Pinto in Minas Gerais, Carlos Lacerda in Guanabara, Juracy Magalhães in Bahia, and Virgílio Távora in Ceará promised a new role for the party, but with the 1962 elections it fell into third place in the chamber of deputies behind the PTB.

The Minor Parties

The eleven minor parties of the 1946 Republic were a mixed bag. Some, such as the Liberation Party (*Partido Libertador* — PL) and the Republican Party (*Partido Republicano* — PR), were throwbacks to the Old Republic of pre-1930. Others represented offshoots of the major parties: the Labor Reform Movement (*Movimento Trabalhista Renovador* — MTR) was organized in 1960 by PTB leader Fernando Ferrari to support his candidacy for vice-president. Another PTB offshoot, the Social Labor Party (*Partido Social Trabalhista* — PST), barely survived between 1946 and 1964.

The Brazilian Socialist Party *(Partido Socialista Brasileiro* — PSB) was originally the Democratic Left of the UDN. It represented socialist intellectual thought and professional groups. It was one of the ideologically oriented parties of the period. Peasant League leader Francisco Julião was a prominent member.

The Christian Democratic Party (*Partido Democrata Cristão* — PDC) was another party with a strong ideological orientation. Created to represent Catholic social doctrine with special emphasis on human dignity and justice, it supported a non-Marxist socialism. It frequently allied with the UDN in elections; its strength rested in São Paulo and Paraná.

The Popular Representation Party (*Partido de Representação Popular* — PRP), a truly ideological party, was the postwar successor to Plínio Salgado's Integralist Party. It claimed to be the first truly nationalist movement in postwar Brazil. In 1955 Salgado's candidacy for president drew 700,000 votes. Salgado was still active in congress in the early 1970s.

The Social Progressive Party (*Partido Social Progressista* — PSP) rose to become the fourth largest party in the chamber of deputies in 1962. Dominated by its personalist leader, Adhemar de Barros, it was a center party, appealing to the urban lower class in the populist tradition of Vargas. De Barros, elected governor in 1947, was reelected in 1962, defeating former President Quadros. He ran for president in 1955 and 1960.

A fourteenth political party, registered in mid-1965, never had time to organize. It was the Good Will Party (*Partido de Boa Vontade* — PBV), which had some support among housewives and lower-class groups in and around the city of Rio de Janeiro.

The Communist Party

Founded in 1922, the Brazilian Communist Party (PCB) has been led since 1935 by Luís Carlos Prestes. Forced underground after the 1935 revolt, the party surfaced in 1945 and sought to keep Vargas in power. The presidential candidate of the party ran third with about 10 percent of the vote in 1945. Prestes was elected to the senate, and fourteen deputies were chosen for the chamber. Four more deputies were added in the 1947 election. The Supreme Electoral Tribunal canceled the party's registration in 1947 when a second set of party statutes was discovered that espoused Marxist-Leninist principles.

After 1947 the PCB ran candidates on other party tickets; it was allowed to propagandize and work fairly openly before 1964. During the 1961-64 period, the party campaigned to have its legality recognized once again. Candidates of the left supported the party's position because they felt its votes would favor them; moderate and conservative leaders spoke out in favor of legalization in order to make the party operate openly. The party was forced underground again in 1964.

The party split in two in 1961 with the formation of a dissident wing favoring violent tactics to overthrow the existing order. The splinter group was known as the Communist Party of Brazil. The new group claimed to favor Peking in the Moscow-Peking division of the world movement and sought to arouse a following among the Northeast Peasant Leagues, students, and intellectuals. Since 1964 the two parties have been involved in a struggle for leadership of the underground opposition against the new terrorist groups that have emerged to harass the Military Republic. These will be discussed in chapter 6. Luís Carlos Prestes remains an active figure in party affairs today.

THE CONGRESS: PARLIAMENTARY FRONTS AND ELECTORAL ALLIANCES

During the 1946-64 period, an increasing number of people were mobilized to participate in the political system. (See Table 10 for data on who voted, 1946-63.) Although the ban against illiterates remained, as it does today, more people were available, with different kinds of demands, for politicalization by populist politicians.

The Brazilian population grew from 41,236,315 in 1940, to 70,119,071 in 1960, to 93,204,379 in 1970, with an estimated growth rate of 2.8 percent (the estimated growth rate of the nineteen Latin American republics is slightly higher).

The urban population grew from 31 percent urban in 1940, to 45 percent in 1960, to 55.9 percent in 1970. The increase in the urban population between 1950 and 1960 is calculated at 70.3 percent, higher than the 57.4 percent average for all of Latin America. In 1960, 32.3 percent of the total population (71.6 percent of the urban population) lived in

Table 10
WHO VOTED, BRAZIL, 1945-63

Year	Population	Registered Voters	% of Pop. Regis.	Actual Vote	% Turnout	% of Pop. Voting
1945 Presidential	46,215,000	7,459,849	16.1	6,200,005	83.1	13.4
1950 Presidential	51,976,000	11,455,149	22.0	8,254,989	72.1	15.9
1954 Legislative	57,098,000	15,104,604	26.5	9,890,475	65.5	17.3
1955 Presidential	58,456,000	15,243,246	26.1	9,097,014	59.7	15.6
1958 Legislative	62,725,000	13,780,244	22.0	12,720,897	92.3	20.3
1960 Presidential	70,967,000	15,543,332	21.9	12,586,354	81.0	17.7
1962 Legislative	75,271,000	18,528,847	24.6	14,747,221	79.6	19.6
1963 Plebiscite	77,521,000	18,565,277	23.9	12,286,173	66.2	15.8

Source: Brazil: Election Factbook, No. 2, September 1965 (Washington, D.C.: Institute for the Comparative Study of Political Systems), p. 19.

urban centers of 10,000 or more inhabitants. And as of 1970, Brazil had four cities with populations of over one million and five other cities with populations of more than half a million people.

The literate population (fifteen years and over) grew from 10,379,990 in 1940, to 24,321,798 in 1960, the percentages for these years being 43.7 and 60.5. In 1940 there were 30,856,325 illiterates; in 1960 there were 45,797,273. The growth rate of the population means that, in absolute terms, Brazil had a larger number of illiterates in the 1960s than in the 1940s.

The pressure that these data represent, combined with the rootless, unstructured party system, led to the progressive disintegration of the parties as autonomous units. In order to win election, thus gaining access to the spoils and patronage available to electoral victors, many candidates and parties formed electoral alliances. Formed by any number of the thirteen political parties active after 1946, the alliances existed only for the sake of electing candidates to office under the proportional representation system employed from 1946 to 1964.[15] They offered no true representation, since candidates elected on an alliance ticket assumed their position in congress as party members — the congress was organized along party, not electoral alliance, lines and in no way heeded the ephemeral affiliation the alliance indicated.

The electoral alliance system reflected the populist tendencies of the post-1946 political system. It indicated the fragility and impermanence of the political party system, the one mechanism that might have overcome the vertical patterns of authority and domination, the continuing political influence of the traditional social and economic elites. The alliance allowed candidates to appeal for votes on the basis of a nebulous promise to improve the lot of the voter without any need of worrying about specific commitments or returns when office had been gained. The voter, having only the electoral system to turn to in his search for leadership and representation, chose among poorly qualified candidates, bewildered by the "na-

[15]See Pompeu de Souza, "Eleições de 1962: Decomposição Partidária e Caminhos da Reforma," *Revista Brasileira de Estudos Políticos,* No. 16 (January, 1964).

Table 11
VOTES AND PERCENTAGES OF VOTE OBTAINED BY MAJOR PARTIES
IN FIVE CONGRESSIONAL ELECTIONS: 1945, 1950, 1954, 1958, and 1962

	PSD	UDN	PTB	Other Parties	Party Alliances	Blank Vote	Total Valid
1945	2,531,944	1,575,375	603,500	1,213,797	—	65,840	5,990,456
%	42.3	26.3	10.1	20.3	—	1.1	100
1950	2,068,405	1,301,459	1,262,000	1,467,804	1,552,636	1,656,909	9,309,213
%	22.2	14.0	13.6	15.8	16.7	17.8	100
1954	2,136,220	1,318,101	1,447,784	1,837,177	2,496,501	468,686	9,704,469
%	22.0	13.6	14.9	18.9	25.7	4.8	100
1958	2,296,640	1,644,314	1,830,621	1,606,828	4,140,655	949,410	12,468,468
%	18.4	13.2	14.7	12.9	33.3	7.6	100
1962	2,225,693	1,604,743	1,722,546	723,509	5,855,692	2,149,111	14,281,294
%	15.6	11.2	12.1	5.1	41.0	15.1	100

Source: Brazil: Election Factbook, No. 2, September 1965 (Washington, D.C.: Institute for the Comparative Study of Political Systems), p. 60.

tional" political party structure between elections and the sudden emergence of "alliances" when it came time to vote.

In the five congressional elections of the 1946 Republic, the percentage of votes cast for alliances rose from 0 percent in 1945 to 16.7 in 1950, to 25.7 in 1954, 33.3 in 1958, and 41.0 in 1962. (See Table 10.) In some states in 1962 the vote on the alliance tickets went as high as 86.2 percent (Espirito Santo) and 89.1 percent (Rio Grande do Norte). The disintegration of the national political party system seemed imminent. The movement away from party candidates toward alliance choices, and the willingness of the parties to subordinate their identity to an ephemeral alliance, indicated the shallowness of both the programmatic content and the ideological dedication of Brazilian parties.

Another manifestation of the weakness of the party system was the emergence in congress of Parliamentary Fronts. Since the parties were unrepresentative of public opinion and cut across class and ideological lines, the political polarization of the 1946 Republic was reflected in the organization of ad hoc groupings in the early 1960s. For example, the National Parliamentary Front (FPN) attempted to galvanize support for "basic reforms" in congress. An ultranationalist radical reform unit, it often accused President Goulart of timidity.

A conservative group, the ADP (Parliamentary Democratic Action) drew its support predominantly from the UDN and attempted to counter the leftist groups at work. And former finance and foreign minister San Tiago Dantas attempted, in 1963-64, to create a Front for Basic Reforms (*Frente Unica*) to lobby for giving the vote to illiterates, legalizing the Communist Party, and reforming labor legislation. It, too, had little success in overcoming the apathy and deep personal divisions that characterized the congress.

THE ELECTORAL SYSTEM

The weak position of the parties in Brazilian politics was further undermined by the electoral system. The chamber of deputies was composed of 409 seats, and deputies were elected for four years by popular election.[16] By the system of proportional representation, each state received one deputy for every 150,000 inhabitants, up to twenty deputies, and then one for each additional 250,000 inhabitants. Each territory was guaranteed one deputy, and the states and federal district a minimum of seven. Alternates were selected from the unsuccessful candidates of each party in the order of the vote received.[17]

There were no congressional districts in the states. All candidates for the chamber ran at large, on a party ticket system. Votes were cast for the individual candidates nominated by the parties, and the total cast for each party's candidates was that party's share of the total vote. Each elector voted for one candidate only. Each party was assigned a number of seats equal to its share of the vote. Once the number of seats allowed the state for each party was decided, the individual candidates received those seats in the order of the votes that they had won.

This system of voting for the chamber — gubernatorial, senatorial, and presidential elections were selected on a direct vote basis — gave overrepresentation to the smaller states. By basing representation on the number of inhabitants rather than on the number of voters, the backward states with high rates of illiteracy and low rates of electoral participation received the same representation as the more heavily populated, urban, participant states in the Center—South.

CONCLUSION

Parties contributed very little to the political life of the 1946 Republic. There was no tradition in Brazil of a strong party system in either the Old or the Transitional Republic. The

[16] Amendment No. 1 to the 1967 Constitution (see chapter 6) reduced the number of seats in the Chamber from 409 to 310. State Assembly seats were reduced to 701 from 1,076. Most important, the basis for deciding the number of seats for each state is now the number of *registered voters* and not the number of inhabitants. This system provides more adequate representation for the more developed states and reduces the overrepresentation of the poorer, underdeveloped states with large numbers of illiterate, illegible voters.

[17] See Ronald H. McDonald, *Party Systems and Elections in Latin America* (Chicago: Markham Publishing Company, 1971), chapter 2, for a more detailed discussion of the electoral system from 1946 to 1964.

organizations of the 1946-64 period were parties in name only. Poorly organized, susceptible to personal and governmental pressure, they were unable to identify an independent policy-making position in the context of the federal congress.

Unable to participate effectively in public policy-making, prevented from adequately representing what was, at best, an amorphous constituency, the parties became dependent creatures, the victims of decisions made by others who little valued their existence and even less mourned their disappearance. Without purpose and without legitimacy, the party system was easily sacrificed by the Military Republic after 1964.

4
The Military and Politics to 1964

In analyzing Latin America Eldon Kenworthy comments that, like much of the Third World, it is "not politically integrated *in the sense that* political institutions do not process the differentiation extant in this set of actors (modern and traditional groups) in such a way that new decisions, societal in scope and reallocative in content, can be implemented." This lack of integration, he continues, may be due to one feature of the operative, as opposed to the stated, rules of the game: the inability of actors to agree on one "currency" for measuring power, "one yardstick by which the various influentials might measure their strength vis-à-vis one another." Two resources, coercion and popularity, are translatable into almost equal quantities of power in Latin America. What is lacking is an acceptable common currency into which the two can be converted, and thus measured, so that decisions can be determined without fear of a veto by the losing groups.[1]

The conflict of the populist politicians, those in possession of "popularity," versus the military, who controlled the means of coercion, characterized the lifespan of the 1946 Republic, giving it its drama. It eventually ended in the military's using their "trump," force, to resolve the confrontation by ousting

[1] Eldon Kenworthy, "Coalitions in the Political Development of Latin America," in Sven Groennings et al., *The Study of Coalition Behavior* (New York: Holt, Rinehart and Winston, 1970), p. 104.

President Goulart.[2] In so doing, the military were fulfilling a traditional role in Brazilian political history: preventing civil disorder and societal disintegration. The qualitative difference in 1964 was that the military determined to exercise public power themselves for the first time since the 1890s by occupying the governmental/bureaucratic offices of the patrimonial regime. Previously, military intervention had occurred to rid the system of a destabilizing influence and had been followed by the return of political control to the civilian elites. In 1964, totally disillusioned with the national experience of civilian government, the military opted for direct rule in an attempt to restore equilibrium to Brazilian society.

In previous political crises, civilian elite groups had attempted to use the armed forces for their own purposes. Thus, the military have always been politicized in Brazil. But, before 1964, there was a widespread belief in the armed forces themselves that they lacked both the ability and the legitimacy to govern. The 1961-64 period "in addition to eroding civilian confidence in the democratic framework of politics, also altered the military officers' previous image of their relative capacity and illegitimacy to rule the country."[3]

A number of causal explanations have been presented in the literature to explain the intervention of the military in politics. The reasons include (1) the numerical size of the military establishment in relation to the size of the civilian population: the larger the armed forces, the easier and more prone they are to intervene to protect their own institutional interests; (2) the desire to thwart communism and internal subversion: civilian governments are more apt to tolerate communist infiltration in the government because of the political support the communists can provide; therefore, the military have the duty to preserve the constitutional system

[2] Dankwart A. Rustow, *A World of Nations* (Washington: The Brookings Institution, 1967), see chapter 6.

[3] Alfred Stepan, *The Military in Politics: Changing Patterns in Brazil* (Princeton: Princeton University Press, 1971), p. 172.

For an excellent treatment of the military and politics see Ronald M. Schneider, *The Political System of Brazil: Emergence of a "Modernizing" Authoritarian Regime, 1964-1970* (New York and London: Columbia University Press, 1971). Schneider is preparing a second volume, *Modernization and the Military in Brazil, 1889-1964.*

from subversion; (3) the goal of nation-building: civilian governments are too often responsive to the oligarchy; the only force willing and able to introduce the measures needed to "modernize" the nation are the military; and (4) because the armed forces are predominantly middle class in social origin, the military will intervene to protect the fragile middle class from the harmful effects of inflation, corruption, or communism. These and other justifications have been used to "explain" military intervention.[4]

Alfred Stepan, in writing about Brazilian military, is correct in stating that "no single factor, institutional or otherwise, taken in isolation can explain or predict political behavior of the military."[5] I have argued elsewhere that "military interventions are but one substantive manifestation of a far deeper phenomenon in developing countries: the general and unavoidable politicization of all social forces and institutions."[6] Given the existence in many countries of praetorian governments — in which civilian institutions lack legitimacy or are in a position to be dominated by the military — it is the larger questions of authority and legitimacy that determine the military's role.

The greater the compliance a regime receives and the greater the support from its subjects, the more legitimate it will be; i.e., its authority will be exercised without frequent resort to force and/or coercion. The less legitimate, the greater the tendency of the military to intervene. As one of the most "politicized" forces in an underdeveloped society, and in Brazil, given their specific historical and constitutional responsibility to protect the nation, the military's intromission in politics is predictable, if not justifiable on normative grounds, when civilian elites have so polarized political opinion that the government cannot function properly. When the very institutional fabric of the regime is in question, the military are

---

[4] See Lyle N. McAlister, "Recent Research and Writings on the Role of the Military in Latin America," *Latin American Research Review*, Vol. 11, No. 1 (Fall, 1966), 5-36.

[5] Stepan, *The Military in Politics*, p. 21.

[6] Riordan Roett, "A Praetorian Army in Politics: the Changing Role of the Brazilian Military," in Riordan Roett (ed.), *Brazil in the Sixties* (Nashville: Vanderbilt University Press, 1972).

inexorably drawn into the partisan fray and ultimately must decide which side will succeed in capturing control of the mechanisms of public power.

In Brazil the military have intervened on numerous occasions since 1889 precisely for these reasons: when the government in office no longer exercised legitimate authority, in the determination of the armed forces, they acted to depose the incumbents and endorse another set of political actors. As the following analysis demonstrates, the roots of Brazilian military intervention are directly tied to the question of political legitimacy and the maintenance, over time, of the basic structure of the bureaucratic-patrimonial state.

THE MILITARY ENTERS POLITICS

After successfully concluding the war against Paraguay in 1870, the Brazilian military did not "unbuckle their swords or relinquish their sense of military never before entering political chambers."[7] Unable to gain satisfaction for their demands from the imperial government, the military toppled the monarchy in 1889 when it became clear that the other major props of the empire — the church and the landowning aristocracy — had withdrawn their support.

The military ruled Brazil from 1889 to 1894. During the period the armed forces assumed the position of guardians of the republic, a position that was confirmed in the Constitution of 1891, and in succeeding documents. A navy revolt in 1893-94 demonstrated the existence of conflicting factions in the armed forces. Basically an intramilitary struggle for leaderships between army and navy, the rebellion was put down by the central government and the army with the help of the São Paulo state militia. In exchange, São Paulo received army support for the election of a Paulista civilian to the presidency in 1894.

The armed forces played an important role behind the scenes in the Old Republic. Not united, the civilian oligarchy

[7] June E. Hahner, *Civilian-Military Relations in Brazil, 1889-1898* (Columbia: University of South Carolina Press, 1969), p. 3.

played one branch against the other. To offset the influence of the army, the Republican government tended to favor the navy's requests for larger appropriations and the latest equipment.[8] In addition, the central government encouraged the creation of state militia with the understanding that they would be at the service of the federal government if challenged by the army. The frequent tension between army and government resulted in frequent denunciations of civilian policy in the *Clube Militar* in Rio de Janeiro. With the victory of the only army officer to occupy the presidency after 1894, Marshal Hermes de Fonseca, civilian oligarchical fears of an increase of the army's influence in politics were confirmed. The following exerpt from a campaign speech of Rui Barbosa, the marshal's opponent in the 1910 presidential campaign, condemns militarism in Brazil:

We have not accustomed [this nation] to fight. Its political traditions are weak. Its republican habits are neglected. Its democracy is composed of humiliations, deceptions, and abdications. Now, in our time, militarism invaded it, corrupted it, mutilated it. The disease has left the organism in a sad condition. In such a state the conspirators count on our regression to a militaristic epoch. Republicans who in the last days of Floriano [Peixoto, president of Brazil from 1891 to 1894] had prevented the declaration of dictatorship with a decided *non possumus* today enlist in its service. Once this is accomplished, Brazil will plunge forever into the servitude of the armed forces, continuous or remittent, periodic or uninterrupted, manifest or disguised, but eternal, organic, incurable.[9]

The involvement of the military in the affairs of the Old Republic increased during and after World War I. While the senior officials defended the existing order by and large, some junior officers reacted unfavorably to the continued elitist domination of the society. Their disorganized protests provided the opening shots of the campaign that defeated the Old Republic.

The *tenentes*, the young army officers who worked for reforms in Brazilian society after World War I, at first confined

[8] Nelson Werneck Sodré, *História Militar de Brasil* (Rio de Janeiro: Editôra Civilização Brasileira, 1965), p. 177-98.

[9] E. Bradford Burns (ed.), *A Documentary History of Brazil* (New York: Alfred A. Knopf, 1966), p. 333.

their campaign to the army itself. Within a short time they sought allies against the Republican Party regime at the local and regional levels. By 1930, when they endorsed Vargas, they had turned to the national level for implementation of their vague but sincere objectives. The *tenentes* revolted in 1922 in Rio de Janeiro and in 1924 in São Paulo. Hoping to combine forces with the São Paulo rebels, Luís Carlos Prestes led his band of followers out of Rio Grande do Sul, where he had been involved in a revolutionary movement. Failing in his goal, with the collapse of the São Paulo resistance, he led his men, the Prestes Column, through the Brazilian backlands in an attempt to incite revolution among the people. Failing to arouse a following, he eventually led his band into Bolivia, having successfully evaded the Brazilian military for two years.

Vargas's rebel army, commanded by Lt. Col. Góes Monteiro, moved on Rio from Rio Grande do Sul. Many military officers and enlisted men had joined its ranks. The northeastern states fell before the challenge posed by Captain Juarez Távora's rebel column. The military commanders in Rio de Janeiro arrested President Washington Luís and formed a junta. That group turned the government over to Vargas on October 24, 1930.

At first Vargas tolerated a diffusion of power in his provisional government. Slowly he consolidated his position, and the senior military officers transferred their allegiance to him. The *tenentes* fragmented; some remained loyal to the president throughout the Transitional Republic. Others became disillusioned with Vargas's authoritarian manner and eventually abandoned his cause. They emerged after 1945 in the opposition to the PSD-PTB coalition.

The military remained an essential underpinning of Vargas's authority from 1930 to 1945. They endorsed his direction of the patrimonial regime when it became clear that he favored a maintenance of the status quo and that the new urban groups he mobilized and aided would not become a destabilizing factor. Vargas carefully placed faithful supporters in positions of influence in the army. General Eurico Dutra became war minister in 1936 and General Góes Monteiro army chief of staff in 1937. Both advocated a strong united army in a well-governed state. They successfully weakened the state militias and actually sought to give the national army a clear monopoly on force.

During Vargas's preparation of his coup in 1937 and the announcement of the New State, the army stood with him. As Thomas Skidmore comments,

... the Army command had been planning on authoritarian solution of Brazil's political crisis since the Communist revolt of November 1935. The higher military were skeptical of Brazil's ability to withstand the confusion and indecision of open political competition, and they were frightened by the prospect of further gains by radicals of the left — who, if ever in power, might succeed in removing the Armed Forces as the ultimate arbiter of political conflict.[10]

With the end of World War II in sight, Vargas promised an opening of the political system. The military, loyal to the regime after 1937, in part due to the large role they were given in the nation's industrial development,[11] understood that it was time for a change. The authoritarian political system of the Transitional Republic would not serve Brazil after the war ended. When Vargas appeared to renege on his promise to hold open elections in December 1945, the military had little compunction in issuing an ultimatum that forced Vargas into retirement. Generals Dutra and Góes Monteiro, the willing supporters of the 1937 coup, masterminded the 1945 ouster. Once again, as in October 1930 and November 1937, the military determined the fate of the nation with limited, if any, significant civilian political input. The growing criticism of the dictator and of his authoritarian government brought into question the legitimacy of the Transitional Republic. Once the military high command decided that Vargas's continuation in power would endanger governmental authority, they acted in their role as constitutional guardians.

THE ARMED FORCES IN THE 1946 REPUBLIC

1945-54, the Military as Guardians

The military presided over the creation of the 1946 Republic. General Góes Monteiro resigned as war minister but

[10]Thomas E. Skidmore, *Politics in Brazil, 1930-1964: An Experiment in*

accepted the new and dominating position of commander-in-chief of the army. The two major candidates were military: Dutra for the PSD and Gomes for the UDN. The civilian politicians looked to the army to guarantee the new political order. The December 1945 election that selected Dutra and the following constitutional assembly that wrote the 1946 document both had army protection.

The Dutra administration maintained the patrimonial system with the superficial trappings of democracy. Decisions were made at the center with a military imprimatur. The elites of the Vargas era, with the PSD as their stronghold, welcomed the relative calm of the placid Dutra administration.

The tensions of 1945 reemerged in 1950 as Getúlio Vargas prepared his campaign for the presidency on the PTB ticket. Although elected to the federal senate in 1945 on the PSD ticket, he used his continuing popularity with the working class to build up the organizational strength of the PTB. Vargas tried to have General Góes Monteiro accept the vice-presidential nomination on his ticket, but he refused, saying he was committed to the Dutra-PSD candidacy.

Vargas accepted the nomination of both the PTB and the PSP parties in 1950. The opposition was divided; both the PSD and the UDN nominated candidates (Brigadeiro Gomes again for the UDN). The army high command remained neutral although unhappy about Vargas's race. His victory in October 1950 opened a four-year period of confusion and chaos in Brazilian politics.

One segment of the military was drawn to Vargas's talk of developmental nationalism.[12] They believed that Brazil had to industrialize to be great, and they were willing to accept Vargas if he provided the necessary leadership for a program of industrialization. Another wing adopted a "wait and see" attitude. If the president did not attempt to upset the balance of social and political forces created in 1946, he could remain in office. If he acted to polarize Brazilian society, he would have

---

Democracy (New York: Oxford University Press, 1967), p. 29.

[11]John D. Wirth, *The Politics of Brazilian Development, 1930-1954* (Stanford: Stanford University Press, 1970).

[12]Skidmore, *Politics in Brazil*, p. 89.

to bear the consequences. A third group maintained its implacable opposition to Vargas and sought ways to undermine his authority.

Although the majority of the armed forces were probably "legalists" in 1950 – they would let Vargas assume office if popularly elected – it is clear that their "protection" was not unlimited. General Góes Monteiro said that Vargas was acceptable as long as he "respected not only the constitution but, in addition, the inalienable rights of the Armed Forces."[13] Although Vargas's war minister, General Estillac Leal, was sympathetic to the leftist nationalists in the armed forces backing the president, he did not speak for all the officer corps.

By 1951, the officer corps was bitterly divided over issues such as the Cold War, communism, and the correct role of foreign capital in the development of national mineral resources. The debate raged in the military clubs and journals. In March 1952 General Estillac Leal had to resign under pressure from the anti-communist, anti-Vargas wing of the military.

Estillac Leal, with support from the military nationalists, decided to stand as a candidate for reelection as president of the Military Club in Rio de Janeiro. An important opinion center for the army, his opposition was a moderate-conservative who favored a "rational nationalism." By almost 2 to 1 Estillac Leal lost his bid for reelection. It was a crushing and public defeat for the extreme nationalists in the officer corps. Vargas took note of the position of the army and moderated somewhat his nationalist program.

By 1954 the economy was in serious difficulty. Inflation and high prices had badly eroded the economic position of the urban groups, the working and middle classes upon whom Vargas had depended for political support. One middle-income group very conscious of its decreasing purchasing power was the officer corps. In February 1954 a group of concerned junior officers protested to the war minister about their low salaries. Many of this group blamed the economic showdown on Vargas's labor minister, João Goulart, Vargas's deputy in PTB-labor politics, who had been appointed in June 1953.

---

[13]Lourival Coutinho, *O General Goes Depoé* ... (Rio de Janeiro: Editôra Coelho Branco, 1955), p. 496.

Military officers feared a continuing decrease in their economic position to satisfy labor's never-ending cry for higher wages and increased benefits. To assuage a rising military discontent, Vargas released Goulart in early 1954. The president could not risk open rebellion among the officer corps; the labor minister was a convenient and acceptable scapegoat.

It can be inferred from Alfred Stepan's research that the majority of the Brazilian army officer corps classifies itself as middle income or "average" in terms of their family's economic status (see Table 12). As important, a large plurality of the officer corps, given Stepan's data on the birthplace of army cadets (see Table 13) come from Guanabara State (41.8 percent), which is the city of Rio de Janeiro. Particularly susceptible to economic fluctuations, the salaried families of Guanabara would be among those hardest-hit by the non-economic performance of the last Vargas years. The officer corps, susceptible to class and kinship ties, were undoubtedly personally aware of their own declining economic position as well as that of friends and family.

Military opposition coalesced around figures such as Generals Juárez Távora and Eduardo Gomes, former *tenentes*, former collaborators of Vargas, and UND candidates for

Table 12
SELF-ASSESSMENT BY BRAZILIAN ARMY ACADEMY CADETS
OF FAMILIES' ECONOMIC STATUS

	1962	1963	1964	1965	1966
Rich	0%	0%	0%	0%	0%
Above average	21	34	26	27	8
Average	70	56	66	66	82
Below average	} 9	} 10	} 8	} 7	8
Poor					2
Total	100%	100%	100%	100%	100%
Number	280	248	244	218	186

Source: From Alfred Stepan, *The Military in Politics: Changing Patterns in Brazil* (copyright © 1971 by the Rand Corporation, published by Princeton University Press), Table 3.4 on p. 36. Reprinted by permission.

president in the 1946 Republic (Gomes in 1945 and 1950; Távora in 1955). The memoranda of the colonels engendered military and civilian criticism of Vargas. It was intolerable that the "guardians of the Constitution" were penurious. In April 1954 the UDN introduced impeachment proceedings in congress when it was alleged that Vargas had been secretly negotiating with President Juan Perón of Argentina over the formation of an anti-United States bloc in Latin America. The motion failed, but clearly the political crisis was deepening.

Table 13
BIRTHPLACE OF ARMY CADETS, 1964-66

State	Total Cadets	State % All Cadets	State Pop. as % of Nat'l. Total	Rough Ratio of Representation
Acre	1	.18	0.2	9/10
Alagoas	6	1.08	1.8	6/10
Amazonas	1	.18	1.2	2/10
Bahia	22	3.95	8.4	5/10
Ceará	20	3.59	4.7	8/10
Espírito Santo	3	.54	1.7	3/10
Goiás	—	—	2.8	—
Guanabara	233	41.83	4.6	90/10
Maranhão	7	1.26	3.5	4/10
Mato Grosso	10	1.80	1.3	14/10
Minas Gerais	57	10.23	13.8	7/10
Pará	6	1.08	2.2	5/10
Paraíba	2	.36	2.8	1/10
Paraná	13	2.33	6.0	4/10
Pernambuco	3	.54	5.8	1/10
Piauí	6	1.08	1.8	6/10
Rio de Janeiro	19	3.41	4.8	7/10
Rio Grande do Norte	4	.72	1.6	5/10
Rio Grande do Sul	80	14.36	7.7	19/10
Santa Catarina	9	1.62	3.0	5/10
São Paulo	46	8.26	18.3	5/10
Sergipe	9	1.62	1.0	16/10
TOTAL	557	100.0	99.0	

Source: From Alfred Stepan, *The Military in Politics: Changing Patterns in Brazil* (copyright © 1971 by the Rand Corporation, published by Princeton University Press), Table 3.5 on p. 38. Reprinted by permission.

Throughout mid-1954 the government drifted; the economy worsened. Vargas's civilian political base had eroded, and his support among the military was limited. Rumors of military coups circulated freely in Rio de Janeiro. Tired and out of contact, Vargas appeared unable to control the deteriorating situation. Suddenly the crisis erupted. A presidential palace-inspired assassination attempt on journalist Carlos Lacerda, a UDN member, failed, but it did kill an air force major. The anti-Vargas military demanded his resignation. On August 22 the president rejected an air force demand for his resignation; then on August 23 the army made the same demand. On August 24, defiantly refusing to resign, Vargas committed suicide, leaving an impassioned letter for the Brazilian people. His conduct assured his immortality in the nationalist pantheon.

1954-64: The Military as Participants

Within the context of the multiparty, competitive system there were military coups in 1954, 1964, an attempted coup in 1961, and the beginnings of a coup in 1955 that brought about a countercoup in defense of the constitutional regime. Each of the real or attempted coups reflected a "crisis plateau" in the development of the 1946 regime. The 1954 coup removed Getúlio Vargas from office once again after his 1950 election as constitutional president. The 1964 coup sent President João Goulart into exile after a stormy three years in office. The 1955 and 1961 coups were both unsuccessful.

The 1955 attempt tried to prevent President-elect Juscelino Kubitschek and Vice-President-elect João Goulart from assuming office. In 1961 the three military ministers unilaterally announced their unwillingness to accept Vice-President Goulart as a successor to President Jânio Quadros, who resigned suddenly after eight months in office. Neither coup had the support of a majority of the military high command or widespread popular support among the civilian political elite. A small segment of the armed forces favored the coups, but without further political justification, the unilateral military decisions were not considered legitimate. The authority of the civilian constitutional order was upheld in spite of the open dissidence of powerful segments of the military establishment.

The 1954 and 1964 coups were political acts with widespread support among the political elite, both civilian and military. These coups also received endorsement from a majority of the participant sectors of the civilian population. The conduct of President Vargas in 1954 and of President Goulart in 1964 provided sufficient justification for a coalescing of civilian-military opinion in favor of their removal from office through military action.

In 1955 the coup was supported by only one of the political parties, the UDN, but the defeated standard-bearers of the party in the election denounced the attempts of their political supporters to subvert the legal order. Such restricted partisan appeals for military force are generally unable to succeed in a praetorian society for fear of a civil war erupting among the major political contenders for power.

The 1961 attempted coup was an immediate reaction by the military ministers which provoked immediate and widespread indignation. They had misjudged the depth of support for the maintenance of the constitutional order by both civilians and military officers. An important factor was the margin of political support provided by the governor of Rio Grande do Sul, Leonel Brizola, the brother-in-law of President Goulart, and the anti-coup sentiments expressed by the commander of the Third Army, located in Porto Alegre, the capital of Rio Grande. The civilian-military elite was unwilling to risk bloodshed to impede Goulart from taking office. Without wider popular and institutional support, the coup was doomed. The military did succeed in limiting Goulart's authority with the imposition of a parliamentary system of government.

These two attempts at coups d'état, 1955 and 1961, indicate the limits of freedom allowed the military establishment. The armed forces, while the most powerful social institution in Brazil, are not the only actors in possession of a power potential. The military, or a coup-prone segment of it, can be thwarted by widespread opposition if it comes from within the military and/or the civilian sector of society.

The 1954 coup removing Getúlio Vargas from office for the second time (which ended in his suicide) was an example of the military's playing its role as moderator in the political system. Vargas had mobilized and manipulated the urban working class throughout his term of office. His populist politics frightened the traditional conservative elites who feared that the president would next turn his attention to the social and economic prerogatives they possessed. Their widespread questioning of presidential authority convinced the military that internal peace required the president's removal. In addition, the widespread stories of corruption and maladministration strengthened the argument against Vargas. The postwar concern of the military with economic growth and technological and industrial development, along with their basic disapproval of populist politics that seemed to represent a threat to law and order, combined to unite the military forces behind Vargas's dismissal.

The 1955 coup grew out of the presidential election of that year. The PSD-PTB ticket was made up of Governor Juscelino Kubitschek of Minas Gerais and former labor minister and PTB leader João Goulart. It was clearly a successor government to Vargas. The UDN nominated General Juarez Távora, an old *tenente* who had broken with Vargas in the 1930s. The PSD-PTB victory had been won with only about a third of the votes cast; Adhemar de Barros and the Social Progress Party (PSP) drew off about 25 percent with his populist campaign reminiscent of Vargas.

The conservative military were furious. Over the cries of these colleagues and UDN politicians who alleged fraud and communist influence, Minister General Henrique Teixeira Lott determined to support the constitution and guarantee the inauguration of the PSD-PTB team. But events moved quickly and Lott's decision appeared unimplementable.

Delivering a eulogy in November 1955 at the funeral of Military Club president General Canrobert Pereira da Costa, who had been war minister under Dutra and an avid opponent of Vargas, Colonel Jurandir Mamede publicly called for military intervention to prevent the inauguration. Once again a polarization of opinion between the pro-legalists and the interventionists occurred. As Lott decided to ask President João Café Filho, Vargas's vice-president who had succeeded him in August 1954, to censure Mamede, Café Filho was hospitalized with a heart attack. The president of the chamber of deputies, Carlos Luz, became acting president. Luz refused to transfer Mamede from his current post. An anti-Kubitschek PSD member, Luz saw little reason to aid a man he had opposed. General Lott resigned as war minister.

All the political parties, except the UDN, publicly opposed a coup. General Távora, the UDN standard-bearer in 1955, was against a coup, but the party remained equivocal. It faced a moral dilemma: to oppose a coup because it contradicted party principles, or to support it and benefit from it? Determined to enforce the election results, General Lott disregarded the UDN and others who were not opposed to a coup. On November 11 he deposed acting president Luz. The congress quickly confirmed its president, Nereu Ramos, as acting president of the republic.

On November 21 President Café Filho left the hospital and prepared to reassume his office. Unwilling to risk disturbing the delicate political balance, the military pressured the congress with the result that Café Filho was disqualified and Nereu Ramos confirmed. The military ministers asked for and quickly received from the congress permission to impose a thirty-day state of siege (a form of martial law). The state of seige was extended in December to run until the inauguration on January 31, 1956.

The Kubitschek years (1956-61) were the quietist politically of the 1946 Republic. By maintaining political stability and a relatively high rate of economic growth, the administration achieved a large degree of legitimacy.[14] By combining nationalism and economic development, Kubitschek received sufficient popular support to ward off any challenge from either civilian or military dissidents.

The military were well treated by Kubitschek, who did not repeat Vargas's error in ignoring the standard of living of officers. Pay raises and new equipment were delivered as requested. General Lott returned to the Government as war minister and effectively maintained a "nonpolitical" stance. The president reassured skeptics who believed him sympathetic to the communists by repeatedly and publicly criticizing them and

[14]See James Rowe, "The 'Revolution' and the 'System': Notes on Brazilian Politics," *American Universities Field Staff Reports Service*, Vol. 12, Nos. 3-5 (1966), East Coast South American Series (Brazil).

by supporting the United States in its Cold War diplomacy.

As a reward, in part, for his defense of Kubitschek and Goulart in 1955, the PSD-PTB coalition turned to General Lott as its presidential candidate in 1960. João Goulart again was nominated for vice-president. The opposition UDN selected Governor Jânio Quadros of São Paulo and Senator Milton Campos of Minas Gerais as their nominees. In the November 1960 election Quadros and Goulart won (the vote for president and vice-president in the 1946 Republic was separate). Both were sworn in without incident in January 1961.

The National War College

An important influence in determining the armed forces' role from 1961 to 1964 was the doctrine of national security (*segurança nacional*) elaborated at the National War College (*Escola Superior de Guerra* – ESG) in the 1950s and early 1960s. Founded in 1949 under the direction of General Cordeiro de Farias, with advice from a United States military mission, the ESG's mission was to prepare "civilians and military to perform executive and advisory functions especially in those organs responsible for the formulation, development, planning and execution of the politics of national security."[15]

The emphasis in the curriculum of the ESG was "the study of basic problems involved in the development of foreign policy and its coordination with the necessities of national security."[16] Both civilians and military officers attended the school's seminars and discussion groups. The civilians were expected to have a university education and to have demonstrated achievement in their profession. Selected by the Armed Forces General Staff, the military officers, normally of colonel or brigadier rank, were approved by the president of the republic. It is estimated that by 1964 two-thirds of the active-duty generals were ESG graduates.

The doctrine of national security that emerged from the seminars and debates of the ESG students emphasized both military security and socioeconomic and political development.

---

[15]Stepan, *The Military in Politics*, p. 176.
[16]Schneider, *The Political System of Brazil*, pp. 244-45.

A National Security Policy and a Development Policy existed in 1964, both of which summarized the needs of Brazil as the ESG perceived them after thorough discussions about the future of the nation among the civilian and military students. By the late 1950s, with the appearance of a rival civilian group in the Institute of Advanced Brazilian Studies (ISEB), who were creating a nationalist-oriented strategy of development, a distinction emerged in the ESG between "national" policy and "government" policy. The former referred to the development and security doctrines of the ESG; the latter identified the specific decisions of the civilian government in power at the moment. By 1964 a wide divergence became evident between the government's position and that of the ESG.[17]

The ESG provided a framework for the armed forces to work with members of the civilian elite to extrapolate a fairly sophisticated conception of Brazil's future development. By combining the issues of military security and national development, very broadly interpreted, the post-1964 civilian and military elites worked together in the years preceding the coup d'état that brought down the Goulart government. A common understanding of the political, social, and economic needs of the nation and a determination to defend the permanent national objectives of Brazil became deeply ingrained in the military through the functioning of the ESG.

After the 1964 coup, the ESG continued to function as an important center for the formation of leaders in the Military Republic. The concept of national security elaborated at the ESG is widely disseminated through the officer corps by the senior officers who have been trained at the school and by the influence of the doctrine in the curriculum of other training courses taken by junior military officers. The esprit de corps of the alumni of the ESG, which has an alumni association and its own magazine, "greatly reenforces the function of the ESG as a vehicle for the co-optation of groups from all social sectors of the elite into the ideological and programmatic outlook of the military technocrats."[18]

By 1964, then, the feelings of inadequacy within the armed forces over their capacity and legitimacy to assume

[17]Ibid., p. 248.
[18]Ibid., p. 250.

power had dramatically decreased. With the support of the civilians with whom they worked, the military were prepared to implement their controversial development doctrine. It called for the maintenance of internal security through well-organized and equipped armed forces, a revision of political institutions and procedures, and central planning for economic and social development. These were basic goals, and the feeling of the armed forces and of their civilian collaborators was that the military alone had the qualities of leadership needed to fulfill the nation's destiny.

1961-64: The Movement toward Intervention

With the sudden crisis of August 1961 and the resignation of Jânio Quadros, the anti-Vargas military were confronted with the possibility of Vargas's heir as president. Would the armed forces sanction the succession of Goulart? Given his absence in Communist China on a trade mission, the president of the chamber of deputies became acting president. It was clear immediately that the military and civilian elites were seriously divided.

The military ministers, led by War Minister General Odílio Denys, opposed Goulart; the legalists favored his inauguration. Acting President Ranieri Mazzilli informed congress on August 28 that "for reasons of national security" Goulart should not return to Brazil. The congress equivocated and recommended that Goulart become chief executive but with reduced powers under a parliamentary form of government.

The military ministers, in a manifesto dated August 29, 1961, reiterated their opposition. Marshal Lott called for Goulart's acceptance and was placed under house arrest by General Denys. The commander of the Third Army in Rio Grande do Sul suddenly proclaimed his support for the vice-president. Was civil war a possibility? Unlike the political crises of 1945, 1954, and 1955, the war minister in 1961 had failed in gathering support for his position from the army field commanders. The Third Army's endorsement of a "legalist" solution — Goulart's succession — deeply divided the armed forces. The war minister, unwilling to risk the unity of the military and bring about a civil war, compromised and accepted the parliamentary compromise. The vice-president arrived in Brasília on September 5, 1961, and took the oath of office two days later.

The Coup of March 31, 1964

The period from September 1961 to March 1964 marked years of crisis in Brazil. The military were deeply divided over the Goulart government. For the first time, the militant nationalist segment of the officer corps received open support from the presidential palace.

Soon after its creation, the parliamentary system proved unworkable. The president's first prime minister resigned in June 1962. His next nominee, San Tiago Dantas of the PTB, was rejected by the congress. PSD senate president Mauro de Andrade, the next nominee, passed the congress but resigned after two days in office. The nation was convulsed by riots and strikes, and inflation was beginning to escalate alarmingly. The military were alert to the possible repercussions of a continuation of the political instability. Finally a PSD deputy from Rio Grande do Sul, received the congress vote as prime minister. The new prime minister, Brochado da Rocha, called for an early national plebiscite on the parliamentary system. The constitutional amendment of September 1961, instituting the parliamentary system, called for a plebiscite in 1965, but the government lobbied for one sooner. Goulart, seeking to assure military support for his plan, transferred nationalist generals into important command posts. The military ministers issued a manifesto in August 1962 supporting an early vote. Congress set the time for April 1963, but Goulart wanted an earlier vote, possibly to coincide with the gubernatorial and congressional elections of October 1962.

Because of its inability to agree on the political strategy to obtain an early plebiscite, the cabinet resigned in September 1962. The succeeding prime minister, Hermes Lima, was a well-known supporter of the vote. The new government removed moderate General Nelson de Melo as war minister and appointed a personal friend of the president, General Amaury

Kruel. The congress finally agreed to set January 3, 1963, as the date of the national plebiscite. With assurances that public order would be maintained, the plebiscite resulted in an overwhelming victory for Goulart, who recovered the full powers of the presidency.

The period from the plebiscite to the coup witnessed increasing polarization in the armed forces. Men such as Generals Nelson de Melo, Odílio Denys, and former Navy Minister (1961) Admiral Sílvio Heck began to plot against Goulart. Strong supporters of the president, such as Generals Osvino Alves and Jair Dantas Ribeiro, received crucial field commands: the First (Rio de Janeiro) and Third (Rio Grande do Sul) Armies respectively. While a majority of the armed forces remained committed to maintaining the constitutional government as long as it did not attempt to radicalize national politics further or suddenly to mobilize mass support that would destabilize the political equilibrium of the 1946 Republic.

Goulart proceeded to do precisely what the moderate military feared. He began to campaign for "basic reforms" in education, housing, the tax system, and land structure. Inflation continued to haunt the government, and in May 1963 a group of officers petitioned Goulart for pay increases, which the congress finally voted in July.

In June 1963 Goulart shuffled his cabinet, appointing as the new war minister General Jair Dantas Ribeiro, commander of the Third Army in Rio Grande do Sul. The nationalists believed they had a stronger spokesman in the new appointee, even though he was a respected officer among his colleagues.

The attempts at economic stabilization had clearly failed by mid-1963. The growing debate over the political direction of the regime had politicized students, labor union members, and peasants. On September 12, 1963, hundreds of noncommissioned officers and enlisted men in the navy, air force, and marines revolted in Brasília. They held the president of the chamber of deputies and a Supreme Court justice prisoner. Though quickly subdued, the incident caused widespread alarm among civilian and military leaders.

In October, Goulart, at the urging of his military ministers, requested approval from congress for a state of siege. The ministers were growing increasingly concerned over their ability to maintain public order. While the congress procrastinated, civilian political opposition to the request grew; suddenly Goulart withdrew the proposal.

Information about a government-inspired military plot to arrest Governor Carlos Lacerda of Guanabara, a vociferous UDN critic of the administration, and Governor Miguel Arraes of Pernambuco, a rival of Goulart on the political left, became public shortly thereafter. While both plans failed, Goulart insisted on disciplining an officer who had refused to participate in the plot against Lacerda.

Senior officers, previously unwilling to believe the president would act unconstitutionally, began to prepare to resist further executive initiatives that they considered illegal. Gradually a large number of officers became convinced that Goulart posed a real threat to public order. The leader of the planners was Army Chief of Staff General Humberto Castello Branco, recently moved out of his command of the Fourth Army in the Northeast (Recife). The challenge to the neutrality of the armed forces that Goulart and his cronies posed deeply concerned the high command. Discipline and hierarchy were under attack; the officer corps was fragmented badly between those supporting and those condemning the chief executive; the mandate that the armed forces held to protect the constitution was being called into question by the leftist, antidemocratic suggestions of reform emanating from the government.

The drift to the left accelerated with the Friday, May 13, rally in Rio de Janeiro where Goulart publicly signed two decrees as part of his new reforms thrust. One nationalized all private oil refineries; the second stated that "underutilized" properties of over 1,200 acres located within six miles of federal highways or railways, and land of more than 70 acres situated within six miles of federal dams, irrigation, or drainage projects would be liable to expropriation. The radicals had won control of presidential policy-making. The themes of the May 13 rally were repeated in Goulart's annual presidential message to congress on March 15. While the left had won the president's ear, it was still a divided left, ranging from the fiery Leonel Brizola, the president's brother-in-law, the "negative" left, to San Tiago Dantas, the "positive" left's leader.

A memorandum by General Costello Branco to his staff, distributed on March 20, convinced many legalist officers that the armed forces had no alternative but to take to the offensive against Goulart. The memorandum confirmed the "historic role" of the military as the defender of the constitutional order and the laws of the nation.

Finally, on the weekend of March 27-29, an issue of military discipline persuaded doubting officers that the time had come for action. The navy minister moved to punish an enlisted sailor who had been actively organizing a labor union of enlisted men. The sailor had been part of the leftist national student organization before his induction. In response to the minister's action, more than one thousand sailors and marines rebelled on March 26 and barricaded themselves in a labor union building in Rio de Janeiro.

Goulart dismissed the navy minister, replacing him with an aged retired admiral who had been endorsed by the General Confederation of Labor, an ally of the radical left. Admiral Paulo Rodrigues, the new minister, offered full amnesty to the rebels. On March 30 Goulart addressed a gathering of sergeants in Rio de Janeiro. Televised nationally, the speech was bellicose in nature; the president refused to separate himself from attacks on military discipline.

The armed forces acted within twenty-four hours. The first troops moved on Rio de Janeiro from Juiz da Fora in Minas Gerais. The civilian UDN governors in Guanabara and Minas Gerais cooperated fully. The troops sent from Rio by Goulart to crush the rebellion joined the rebels. Appeals by Goulart for popular demonstrations of support failed, and he fled from Rio to Brasília and then to Porto Alegre in Rio Grande do Sul. The president of the senate declared the presidency vacant the same night; the president of the chamber of deputies, following the constitutional directive, became acting president.

CONCLUSION

The military intervened to remove President Goulart because he had attempted to utilize "popularity" to offset the potential "coercion" of the armed forces. Once again, when the military decided that the chief executive had attempted to change the operating rules of the game — thereby violating the constitution, disrupting the "civic tranquility" of the nation, and undermining the neutrality and effectiveness of the military establishment — they acted collectively to remove him from office and restore the status quo ante.

Undoubtedly the growing dissatisfaction of the middle class, buffeted by hyperinflation, and increasing food and transportation costs, influenced the course taken by the armed forces; but the fact that they were of middle-class origin did not mean they necessarily acted on behalf of the middle class, as José Nun has argued.[19] As a national institution, imbued with a historic sense of responsibility toward the constitution, the armed forces view themselves as acting independently of any one class for the benefit of all classes. Such is the intent, if not always the outcome, of their political intervention.

In the opinion of a majority of the officer corps, João Goulart no longer exercised legitimate authority in 1964. He had begun to act extraconstitutionally, to threaten reform without congressional participation, to erode military discipline without adequate explanation, and to mobilize students and laborers for direct political action. All this threatened to undermine the fragile institutional structure of the 1946 Republic. The military acted to preserve and restore the bureaucratic-patrimonial state before it was severely weakened by Goulart, who did not appear to have a viable alternative to substitute in its place. The pressure of the stalwarts of the patrimonial regime, Goulart's political ineptness and bombast, and the military's tortured realization that their ability to act would be hampered by the left's campaign to destroy military discipline, resulted in the coup d'état of March 31, 1964.

The armed forces came to believe, by 1964, that they possessed a constitutional mandate to remove Goulart from office. The constitutions of 1891, 1934, and 1946 stated that the military existed as a national institution with the responsibility of maintaining public order and guaranteeing the normal functioning of the three branches of government. But the constitutions also stipulated that while the military were

---

[19]José Nun, "The Middle-Class Military Coup," in Claudio Veliz (ed.), *The Politics of Conformity in Latin America* (New York: Oxford University Press, 1967).

subordinate to the chief executive, their obedience was binding only when the president acted within the limits of the law. In the final analysis, the military held the discretionary power to determine whether or not the chief executive was acting within the constitution.

In addition, the stimulus that the development doctrines of the ESG provided motivated the armed forces to reconsider their previous unwillingness to assume power. Given the inability of the Goulart government to progress in its reform program — which many officers doubted was either sincere or appropriate — the ESG alumni came to believe that their program was superior to that of the administration in power. With the support of key civilian groups, possessed of a doctrine of development, and convinced that they could effectively govern Brazil themselves, the armed forces assumed power.

5

The Patrimonial State and Society in Brazil

In discussing the functioning of the patrimonial state, we have noted the weakness and ineffectiveness of the political party system. Besides the party organizations, other groups have suffered a similar fate: the inability to oppose the interests of the central government and still survive. Groups and institutions seeking to maneuver within the restrictions of Brazil's patrimonial regime learn to cooperate or to allow themselves to be co-opted; otherwise they confront unmitigating hostility. In this chapter we will examine the role of students, the church, industrial groups, and labor to demonstrate the centrality of our argument that any institution or group attempting to disturb the social and political status quo has little, if any, chance of success as long as the armed forces continue to occupy the key decision-making roles in Brazil. As well, we will examine the bureaucracy and its role in maintaining the patrimonial state.

In analyzing "interest conflict and political change in Brazil" Philippe Schmitter comments:

Continuity has been sustained by persistent infusions of paternalism, co-operation, and anticipated reaction. As a result, primary emphasis and responsibility are given to the legal and administrative machinery of the state for the regulation of social conflict and the sponsorship of social improvements, and spontaneous conflicts between group forces are regarded with suspicion or outright alarm. Thus desire for controlled change from above is crucial to the authoritarian corporatist response to development.[1]

[1] Philippe C. Schmitter, *Interest Conflict and Political Change in Brazil* (Stanford: Stanford University Press, 1971), pp. 380-81.

111

Schmitter states also that "a history of paternalism and patrimonialism has made association leaders and followers ready to leave initiation to higher authorities and to regard the government as the supreme patrão of the society."[2] The willingness to "leave it to the state," the lack of interest group activity — Martin Needler has mentioned "the weakness of such intermediary structures" in Latin American political processes,[3] and the "corporatist" nature of Brazilian society — the "belief in and acceptance of a natural hierarchy of social groups, each with its ordained place and its own set of perquisite responsibilities,"[4] all confirm the continuing reality of the patrimonial order in Brazilian society.

The groups that we examine here are all interrelated in the context of the 1946 Republic and the events leading to the 1964 Revolution. After 1945 the Church became caught up in the international movement of Roman Catholicism toward greater social involvement. In Brazil, Church and students converged in their desire to see society change. While the emphases and programs were often unrelated, there was a core concern motivating their conduct. The postwar industrialization growth of Brazil created a new group, the industrialists, who were prevented from assuming an autonomous political role because of restraints imposed by the patrimonial political system. The laboring and peasant classes became the center of attention of one phase of Catholic activism in those years as the unionization effort among the rural workers gained momentum in 1963 and 1964. These groups represented a new dimension of the development process in Brazil. And all had a similar, if not exact, fate after March 31, 1964.

THE ROMAN CATHOLIC CHURCH

Frank Bonilla has stated that "the military and the Church lay claim, in part justifiably, to being the only genuinely national institutions" in Brazil. The Church believes, he continues, "itself the receptacle and instrument of a moral and

---

[2] Ibid., p. 362.

[3] Martin C. Needler, *Political Development in Latin America: Instability, Violence, and Evolutionary Change* (New York: Random House, 1968), p. 47.

[4] Schmitter, *Interest Conflict*, p. 98.

spiritual unity that binds Brazilians together in ways that political loyalties have never matched."[5] After the victory of the March 31, 1964 movement, the Church found itself the only institution with the autonomy and resources to criticize the military regime publicly. The first years after the Revolution of 1964 saw the Church in opposition; the later years, with a few bold and dramatic exceptions, have seen the instinct for survival surface and dictate a rapprochement with the patrimonial regime.

Background

The Church in Brazil, during the Empire, provided one of the principal supports for elitist, monarchical rule. With the Republic in 1889, church and state were separated. During the Old Republic, the Church operated freely without governmental interference. In a nation in which more than 90 percent of the population are members, the Church continued to play an important social and educational role.

With Vargas's victory in 1930, the archbishop of Rio, Cardinal Leme, informally renegotiated many of the prerogatives the Church had previously enjoyed. The 1934, 1937, and 1946 Constitutions refer to God in the preambles, and the provisions relating to marriage and education explicitly recognize the preeminent place of Roman Catholicism. Members of the clergy enjoy full political rights and many have served in the congress. Informal ties between church and state continue particularly in the health, education, and social welfare areas. It is a necessary and expected aspect of all state ceremonies that a ranking member of the clergy attend and participate in the ceremonies. Thus, Brazil remains a deeply Catholic country, not measured by church attendance, but by the respect and projection into society that the Church enjoys.

The Church Modernizes

Only after 1945 did segments of the Church begin to

---

[5] Frank Bonilla, "Brazil," in James S. Coleman (ed.), *Education and Political Development* (Princeton: Princeton University Press, 1965), p. 216.

assume a more militant role regarding social and political questions. The issue of the Church as an institution versus the Church as a movement was deeply debated. Its institutional need

> entails an intrinsic involvement with politics that often leads to cautious, generally conservative positions on most political questions . . . this involvement has frequently led to the Church's "sacrilizing" tradition and becoming a key element in social control and norm maintenance by its conferral of religious legitimacy on established social structures and authority patterns.[6]

Those who emphasize the Church's social, missionary role see the hierarchical and material aspects of its existence as a barrier. Ivan Vallier has called those concerned with preservation of the present internal structure and in favor of a policy supportive of the state, regardless of its social position, the "politicians." Today the Brazilian Church is divided between the politicians and the other three elites in the Church: the "papists" who stand for a modern and militant Catholicism, the "pastors" who seek to create strong, worship-centered congregations, and the "pluralists" who favor "grass-roots ethical action in the world." Vallier sees Brazil as the center of a strong pastor-pluralist movement.[7]

After 1945 the writing of the French left deeply influenced activist Catholics, particularly the work of Jacques Maritain, Emmanuel Mounier, and the French Dominican priest, L.B. Lebret. The need to bring the Church into the twentieth century was recognized in Rome. The Latin American Episcopal Conference, created in 1955 to analyze Latin American problems, was followed in 1958 by the organization of the Papal Commission for Latin America. The National Conference of Brazilian Bishops (CNBB) had been founded in 1952 with Bishop Hélder Câmara as its secretary-general.

The international church became more activist with the

---

[6] Luigi Einaudi et al., *Latin American Institutional Development: The Changing Catholic Church* (Santa Monica: The Rand Corporation, 1969), p. 47.

[7] Ivan Vallier, "Religious Elites: Differentiations and Developments in Roman Catholicism," in Seymour M. Lipset and Aldo Solari (eds.), *Elites in Latin America* (New York: Oxford University Press, 1967), p. 203.

hn XXIII in 1958. The influence of the
ne of the "supranational actors" that
fies as important in Latin America,[8]
1 assessing the development of the
XXIII's encyclicals, *Mater et Magistra*
in in Terris (1963), and the meeting of Vatican
II (1962) all provided important support for indigenous
Catholic forces convinced that the Brazilian Church, to survive,
must become relevant to the needs of the poor.

The CNBB, under Hélder Câmara's influence, became
increasingly vocal in analyzing outstanding social issues. The
Church was instrumental in supporting the creation of the
Superintendency for the Development of the Northeast
(SUDENE) in 1959. Church action groups in the Northeast had
been expanding the Church's role for a number of years before
Juscelino Kubitschek announced, at a regional meeting organized by the CNBB, that the federal government would actively
seek to resolve the extraordinary misery of the nine-state area.

The pastoral letters of the Brazilian bishops issued in 1962
and 1963 reflected the newfound social calling. One such
document, issued in 1962, was an "Emergency Plan" of the
CNBB for the Church in Brazil. Hélder Câmara served also as
national secretary of the Catholic Action Movement during
these years. His spirit of innovation permeated the youth
movements, particularly the Catholic University Student Organization (JUC), which became a leading proponent of radical
Catholic action.

The concern of the students in JUC focused on making
existing institutions more responsive to the needs of national
development. JUC actively participated in the formation of
Popular Action (AP) in 1962, a new, radical Roman Catholic
action group. *Brasil Urgente,* the radical Catholic paper published in 1963 and 1964, publicized the platform of change AP
advocated. AP was not a church-affiliated entity, as Catholic
Action was. It was a "political-ideological" and "nonconfes-
sional" organization that hoped to attract all Catholics in Brazil

[8] Charles W. Anderson, *Politics and Economic Change in Latin America: The Governing of Restless Nations* (Princeton: D. Van Nostrand, 1967).

committed to change.[9] The radical Catholic movem
penetrated the National Union of Students (UNE) and
communist student backing, succeeded in electing four p
dents in a row prior to 1964.

The increasing militancy of AP deeply enraged "tradition
al" Catholics. Its identification with the "basic reform"
movement of the Goulart administration disturbed the military.
As the 1963-64 crisis mounted, the Church organized peasant
unions in the Northeast; it sponsored, through the Basic
Education Movement (MEB), a program of rural education
reaching 180,000 peasants over twenty-five radio stations. The
MEB approach utilized the work of Paulo Freire, who combined
literacy education with *conscientização*: instilling in the peasant
a consciousness of his condition and his rights.

MEB had been organized in March 1961 as a collaborative
effort of the CNBB and the Brazilian government to utilize
radio education to reduce illiteracy among the people of the
underdeveloped regions of the country. President Quadros had
been impressed by the radio education programs initiated in the
late 1950s in Natal, Rio Grande do Norte, and Aracajú, Sergipe,
as part of the Church's social awakening. The Church agreed to
organize the program, and the government financed it.

The radio schools spread throughout the North and
Northeast from 1961 to 1964. Organized by the CNBB, the
MEB became an independent agency directed nationally by a
Council of Bishops appointed by the CNBB. A good deal of
autonomy was allowed, and encouraged, at the state and local
levels. The Movement began to move towards a more radical
position in late 1962. Adopting the theme of *conscientização*
and social action, MEB prepared a controversial textbook,
Vivar É Lutar (To Live Is to Struggle) in 1963, which, when
printed in January 1964, was seized by Governor Carlos
Lacerda of Guanabara because it was communist-inspired, in
his opinion.

The Movement's potential for making a real contribution
to social awareness in the countryside was cut short by the
1964 coup. While not banned officially, the MEB received no

[9] Thomas G. Sanders, "Catholicism and Development: The Catholic Left in
Brazil," in Kalman H. Silvert (ed.), *Churches and States: The Religious Institution
and Modernization* (New York: American Universities Field Staff, 1967), p. 95.

encouragement from the government and its lay leaders were persecuted. The network of stations dwindled to a few dozen by the late 1960s.

One of the principal instigators of *conscientização*, as an instrument for attacking illiteracy and social deprivation, was Professor Paulo Freire of the University of Recife. The *Método Paulo Freire* (Paulo Freire Method) stressed relevance and equality in its teaching methods. The vocabulary to which the peasant or worker was exposed was drawn from his own experience and related to his social and political needs. There were no "teachers," in the traditional sense, in the courses organized by Freire and his followers. "Coordinators" guided the literacy classes, but every effort was made to equalize relations among all the participants, instructors and students alike.[10]

Freire used the Cultural Extension Service of the University of Recife to administer the program. Attracting a vigorous and dedicated group, primarily university students and instructors and intellectuals, he had hopes of reaching millions of illiterate Brazilians with his dynamic method of learning. Unfortunately, the 1964 coup intervened; Freire went into exile in Chile.

Another instrument of *conscientização*, in this period before 1964, was the *Movimento de Cultura Popular* (Movement of Popular Culture) or MCP, which also attracted strong radical Catholic support as well as the aid of the Communist Party. An important MCP center opened in Recife under Mayor Miguel Arraes in 1960. In its early days, Paulo Freire had cooperated with the Recife program but moved to the Cultural Extension Service as the MCP came under increasing criticism as a subversive organization. *Cultura Popular* (Popular Culture) programs were espoused by a number of student and Church-related groups.[11] Plays, outdoor assemblies, pamphlets, and films were used to arouse the masses. At a congress held in Recife in September 1963, one delegate stated the movement's purpose as follows:

[10]See Paulo Freire, *Educação Como Prática da Liberdade* (Rio de Janeiro: Editôra Paz e Terra, 1967).

[11]Emanuel de Kadt, *Catholic Radicals in Brazil* (London and New York: Oxford University Press, 1970), p. 105.

Cultura Popular assumes the character of a struggle. Apart from forming an authentic national culture, this struggle promotes the integration of Brazilian man in the process to socio-economic and politico-cultural liberation of our people.[12]

The ideology of the MCP spread through Brazil with the opening of Popular Centers of Culture. Dominated by Marxists, with varying degrees of support from the Catholic radicals, the movement was closed down by the military in 1964 with little substantive success to show for its efforts.

With the coup d'état of 1964, the military quickly shuttered AP, JUC, UNE, MEB, and other radical Catholic and popular organizations; their leaders were imprisoned and exiled; their programs condemned as subversive and "anti-Brazilian." With the disappearance of the student and laity groups, only the Church itself remained to carry on the struggle.

The leader of the Church "resistance" to the authoritarian rule of the Military Republic became Dom Hélder Câmara, appointed archbishop of Recife and Olinda at the time of the 1964 Revolution. As the spiritual leader of the major archdiocese in the most underdeveloped area in the hemisphere, Hélder Câmara fought to keep the "movement" alive. Advocating nonviolent action, he organized the Movement for Action, Justice, and Peace; it became inactive after Institutional Act No. 5 in December 1968. Long a target of the right wing in Brazil, one of his priests was brutally murdered in May 1969 by, it is suspected, the CCC (the Command to Hunt Down the Communist). The archbishop is supposedly on their list for elimination.

By the 1970s Hélder Câmara spent as much time outside of Brazil as he did at home. He carried the message of militancy to the outside world, condemning the political imprisonments and tortures of the regime and the lack of progress on social reform. Despised by the armed forces hierarchy and by traditional Catholics, he remains the best-known prelate in Brazil and perhaps the hemisphere.

The national church has had to steer a delicate line between social advocacy and institutional survival since 1964. The national hierarchy has spoken out against the government when priests and nuns have been arrested and tortured for

[12]Einaudi et al., *Latin American Institutional Development*, Section II.

political activities. The greatest period of tenseness occurred from 1964 to 1967 when the clergy supported the growing militancy of the university students. Priests have been involved in the clandestine meetings of UNE and the guerrilla kidnappings of diplomats. In Novemner 1967 the Central Commission of the CNBB issued a document entitled "Why the Bishops Cannot Remain Quiet," which criticized government policies. In August 1967 an open letter to the bishops from three hundred local priests emphasized the divisions in the clergy between the moderates and the progressives.

Pope Paul VI's encyclical in 1967, *Populorum Progresso* ("On the Development of Peoples") and his visit to Bogotá, Colombia, in 1968 to address the Second General Conference of CELAM gave renewed impetus to the responsibility of the Brazilian Church in the area of social reform. That message has served to justify the continued attempts of the progressive clergy to make the patrimonial order more responsive to the needs of the poor. At the same time such efforts have aroused hostility and, at times, violent opposition of groups such as the CCC and the TFP ("Society to Defend Tradition, Family, and Propriety") located in São Paulo. The TPF, an organization of conservative Catholic youth, has as its objective the purification of the church by ridding it of radical influence.

The Church in Brazil has come to make its peace with the patrimonial regime; it is confronted with staggering problems. The total religious personnel equalled 52,566 in 1968. In terms of the number of priests per 10,000 population in 1968, Brazil ranked thirteenth in Latin America, with 14/10,000, the lowest-ranking of all the major nations. The recruitment rate is very low for new religious. Pentecostal Protestantism and Spiritualism attract a growing number of converts annually.[13] The rural areas, in which the need for the reform militancy of the church is most obvious, have few priests. Dominated by what Emanuel de Kadt calls "Folk Catholicism," which is heavily influenced by the African cults and local religious habits of the backlands,[14] the backlands are "Catholic" in name only.

[13]Emilio Willems, *Followers of the New Faith* (Nashville: Vanderbilt University Press, 1967).

[14]Emanuel de Kadt, "Religion, the Church, and Social Change in Brazil," in Claudio Veliz (ed.), *The Politics of Conformity in Latin America* (New York: Oxford University Press, 1967), pp. 192-220.

The symbolic reconciliation of church and state took place in May 1970. The XI General Assembly of the CNBB, meeting in Brasília, issued a document entitled *Pastoral de Brasília* summarizing the assembly's deliberations. The government clearly welcomed and endorsed the mild tone of the document, which did not condemn the regime but exhorted it to work for the good of all Brazilians.

The assembly was followed immediately by the opening in Brasília of the VIII National Eucharistic Congress. The cardinal archbishop of Salvador, Dom Eugênio Sales, served as the papal legate or representative. He was greeted, on his arrival in the capital, by President Médici and given the honors due a chief of state. The government participated prominently in the congress, hosting a formal luncheon for the papal representative and a delegation of bishops.[15]

To preserve any portion of its freedom as a "movement," the Church in Brazil has decided to safeguard its position as an "institution"; the political realities of today's Brazil dictate collaboration and not conflict between church and state. This does not signify a "betrayal" by the Church of its duty to work to improve the life of its people. It means that the Church recognizes the power and authority of the patrimonial order and cannot afford to destroy its credibility and projection in Brazil, in the long run, with short-term harassment and negative criticism. Caught between two conflicting roles, the Church selected the one it felt best suited to its preservation. In choosing that course, the only effective and independent force perhaps capable of ameliorating the impact of the military regime withdrew from confrontation.

UNIVERSITY STUDENTS

Kalman Silvert comments that the impact of students on politics is "in inverse relation to the strength of governments and the efficacy of the university administrations themselves. The relative influence of organized student movement must be heightened by the essential fragility of societies in transition

---

[15]*Jornal do Brasil* (Rio), May 28, 1970.

toward modern nationhood."[16]

And Samuel Huntington has written that "in praetorian societies students are typically the most active and important civilian middle-class political force."[17] Both of these comments represent the status of university students in Brazil. During the 1946 Republic the national student movement became an extremely voal advocate of radical societal reform. Given the praetorian status of Brazilian society, student groups dramatically focused attention on the issues of nationalism and development. Because of the institutional weakness of the Goulart administration and the rapidly growing clamor for structural changes, the 1961-1964 years were the most active and influential for the student movement. Since 1964, the students have actively opposed the military but without the public projection they achieved in supporting the ephemeral radical reform movement of João Goulart.

Background

Unlike Spanish America, where universities were founded at Lima, Mexico City, and Santo Domingo in the middle of the sixteenth century, "the Jesuit colleges were almost the only centers of intellectual culture in Brazil during its three centuries of colonial life."[18] They served the colonial aristocracy: the curriculum "was neither popular nor vocational, for it only had in view the humanistic and catholic formation of the ruling classes."[19] For further education, children were sent to Portugal or France. With the expulsion of the Jesuits by Pombal in 1759, even elite education collapsed.

Several higher educational institutions were created by Dom João VI after the arrival of the Portuguese court in 1808. During the Empire the illiteracy rate among the Brazilian

[16]K.H. Silvert, "The University Student," in Peter G. Snow (ed.), *Government and Politics in Latin America* (New York: Holt, Rinehart and Winston, 1967), p. 368.

[17]Samuel P. Huntington, *Political Order in Changing Societies* (New Haven and London: Yale University Press, 1968), p. 369.

[18]Robert J. Havighurst and J. Roberto Moreira, *Society and Education in Brazil* (Pittsburgh: University of Pittsburgh Press, 1965), p.55.

[19]Ibid., p. 56.

population never fell below 85 percent; the meager educational opportunities of Imperial Brazil remained the private domain of the privileged.

The first university was organized in Rio de Janeiro in 1920 by combining the schools of law, medicine, and engineering. The University of Rio de Janeiro became the University of Brazil in 1938; the University of São Paulo, a state institution, opened in 1934. By 1967 Brazil had thirty-eight universities, the second greatest number in Latin America (Mexico had fifty-six), but only the Universities of Rio de Janeiro and São Paulo had enrollments higher than 10,000 students (11,000 and 11,900 respectively). Of the 831,400 students enrolled in institutions of higher learning, 158,000 were in Brazil (compared to 256,000 in Argentina and 128,000 in Mexico).[20]

The weekly news magazine *Visão* in an article published in 1968, commented that nothing had happened in the preceding ten years in Brazilian education: "nothing changed, or, if it moved, it became worse."[21] Extensive coverage by *Visão* in 1958 about education, the article said, could be repeated verbatim in 1968.

As Douglas Graham has pointed out, university enrollment in the 1960s increased more than at the primary and secondary level (see Table 14), and university enrollment itself was rapidly increasing (see Table 15).[22] While the percentage of the Gross Domestic Product spent on education increased from 2.4 percent in 1960 to 3.8 percent in 1969 and 1970, "with reference to higher education it is possible that, due to the remarkable rise in enrollments during the decade, the expenditure per student has been declining significantly while the expenditure GNP ratio for higher education may have been rising."[23] It is the frustration of the university student over the lack of change in the university curriculum, the self-image of the student as a reformer, and the opportunities for dissent and activism in a society with weak institutions and low levels of

[20]*Socio-Economic Progress in Latin America* (Washington: Inter-American Development Bank, 1967).

[21]"Dez Anos Depois: Continua Ruim," *Visão*, August 16, 1968.

[22]Douglas H. Graham, "The Growth, Change and Reform of Higher Education in Brazil in the Sixties: A Review and commentary on Selected Problems and Issues," in Riordan Roett (ed.), *Brazil in the Sixties*, p. 8.

[23]Ibid., p. 18.

Table 14

PERCENTAGE INCREASE OF ENROLLMENTS IN BRAZIL
FOR SELECTED YEARS

| | Level of Education | | |
	Elementary	Secondary	Higher
1950/60	71.4	118.7	117.0
1960/68	65.4	172.3	195.4

Source: Douglas H. Graham, "The Growth, Change and Reform of Higher Education in Brazil in the Sixties: A Review and Commentary on Selected Problems and Issues," p. 8 in Riordan Roett (ed.), Brazil in the Sixties (Nashville: Vanderbilt University Press, 1972).

Table 15

PERCENTAGE INCREASE OF ENROLLMENT FOR HIGHER
EDUCATION IN BRAZIL FOR SELECTED PERIODS

1965/66	15.5
1966/67	18.3
1967/68	31.3
1960/65	64.5
1965/68	79.5

Source: Douglas H. Graham, "The Growth, Change and Reform of Higher Education in Brazil in the Sixties: A Review and Commentary on Selected Problems and Issues," p. 8 in Riordan Roett (ed.), Brazil in the Sixties (Nashville: Vanderbilt University Press, 1972).

political legitimacy that have motivated Brazilian students. Alistair Hennessey is correct in stating that "it is unrealistic to expect students to eschew politics and embrace a new professionalism based on the needs of a technical revolution so long as they are enmeshed in an outworn and unreformed university system."[24]

The Students Organize

The Brazilian student was "a nationalist, a propagandist, an agitator, and a reformer" in colonial days, and he and his colleagues were "enthusiastic liberals, nationalists, and federal-

[24] Alastair Hennessy, "University Students in National Politics," in Veliz (ed.), The Politics of Conformity in Latin America, p. 119.

ists" in the early empire.[25] Later they backed the abolition of slavery and of the monarchy itself. Students opposed the Old Republic and endorsed the *tenentes* and the Liberal Alliance of Vargas in 1930. Their support for Vargas lasted for a brief time only; by 1932 and the São Paulo rebellion, the students were in opposition to authority again.

The Transitional Republic patronized the student movement and attempted to co-opt it through financial subsidies. The National Union of Students (UNE) was organized in 1937 at the instigation of the *Estado Novo*. It was an organization without structure, and only in the following ten years was a national student movement created, consisting of centers and directories in individual faculties or schools. UNE became the principal center of national student political activity.

The Communist Party actively participated in student politics in the first years of the 1946 Republic. The party dominated UNE until 1952; from 1952 to 1956 more moderate student groups succeeded in controlling the organization. After 1956 students' politics grew more radical. The communists returned to play an important role, often in alliance with the radical Catholic student groups such as Catholic University Youth (JUC) (1959-1961) and Popular Action (AP) (1961-1964).[26]

By early 1964, Popular Action controlled UNE and student politics. One commentator wrote that

the AP is an elite organization and few students are actually recruited into the organization. National membership is estimated to be between 2000 and 3000 active members. Their voting strength is much greater, of course. Presently, [early 1964] they dominate the majority of Brazil's 500 plus faculties, most of the 22 state unions, and enjoy a controlling voice on the directorate of the National Union of Students.[27]

The student movement, directed by the JUC-AP and Communist Party-affiliated students, supported Goulart's basic reform drive. They condemned United States foreign invest-

[25]Robert O. Myhr, "The University Student Tradition in Brazil," *Journal of Inter-American Studies and World Affairs,* Vol. 12, No. 1 (January, 1970), 129-30.

[26]Leonard D. Therry, "Dominant Power Components in the Brazilian University Student Movement Prior to April, 1964," *Journal of Inter-American Studies,* Vol. 7, No. 1 (January, 1965), 27-48.

[27]Ibid., p. 35.

ment and the exploitation of the peasantry by the landowning oligarchy; they favored a widespread literacy program and actively sought to unionize the *campesinos* in the rural sector. At the first meeting of the CONTAG (National Confederation of Agricultural Workers) in December 1963, AP-MEB rural union leaders joined the communist-oriented unions to defeat the Catholic Church-inspired unions.

With the Revolution, UNE headquarters were burned and UNE leaders imprisoned or driven into exile or underground. In October 1964, congress approved the abolition of UNE by a vote of 126 for, 117 against, 5 abstentions (called the "Lei Suplicy" after the incumbent education minister). A National Student Directory (DNE) was substituted. The UNE and state student unions lost legal monopoly over student representation granted by the *Estado Novo* in 1942 as well as the legal guarantee of internal autonomy awarded in 1955. The DNE and its state affiliates were forbidden from participating in political activities. DNE headquarters moved to Brasília from Rio; only the minister of education could authorize plenary meetings; the federal subsidy provided was to be inspected carefully by the Federal Education Council; and DNE elections were given to the university administrations to control.

UNE and most state unions rebelled. Abolished legally, without funds, harassed by state and federal authorities, a general congress still met in July 1966 in a Franciscan convent in Belo Horizonte. Radical students and priests began to work with and join the terrorist groups that began to harass the regime. Students became increasingly violent. In April 1968, in a tragic incident in Rio, a university student was shot and killed. The resulting demonstrations were met with severe force by the government. The DNE was abolished by the government when it became clear that students would not support it.

After the Fifth Institutional Act of December 1968, student opposition went underground. The growing authoritarianism of the patrimonial regime allowed no room for dissent. The Médici government, through its education minister, attempted to involve students in discussing educational reform by forming a student advisory group of six students. But the reaction to that initiative was negative. Fifty-six percent of the three hundred students asked in a *Veja* survey if they supported the idea said no; 59 percent replied that the new group was not sufficient to give students power to influence the government's education policy.[28]

The national student movement in Brazil has disappeared. But there is little reason to believe it has been eradicated for, as Samuel Huntington has stated:

The student opposition to government represents the extreme middle-class syndrome of opposition because it is so constant. Student opposition can only be marginally influenced by reforms of ameliorative government actions. It exists virtually independent of the nature of the government in the society and of the nature of the policies which the government pursues.[29]

The present hiatus in student activism will last only as long as the regime suppresses it forcibly.

INDUSTRIAL GROUPS

Writing about the continuing inability of industrial groups to exert pressure on government policy-making in postwar Brazil, Nathaniel Leff comments that, because of Brazilian political culture,

... *all* pressure groups are placed at a disadvantage ... the claims of interest groups have little legitimacy, for they are distrusted as selfish and are discounted heavily because of their obvious "egoism." In a system of elite politics where prestige and moral authority count for a great deal, therefore, "special" interests are at a severe disadvantage.[30]

It is the dominant role of the patrimonial state that has determined economic policy in Brazil throughout the nineteenth and twentieth centuries. Unlike the earlier industrial societies, both the freewheeling role of entrepreneurship and the give-and-take of competitive, pluralistic politics has bypassed Brazil.

A tradition of government protection of, and intervention

[28] *Veja* (Rio), April 22, 1970, p. 65.
[29] Huntington, *Political Order*, p. 369.
[30] Nathaniel Leff, *Economic Policy-Making and Development in Brazil, 1947-64* (New York: John Wiley & Sons, 1968), p. 113.

in, economic affairs began with the agricultural producers of the nineteenth century, particularly the coffee planters of São Paulo. The government manipulated exchange rates and devised price support programs to maintain prices in the face of overproduction. Similar policies were instituted for the uneconomic sugar producers of the Northeast coast.

The interventionism of the government in the industrial sector began with the cotton textile industry in the last half of the nineteenth century. "Creeping protection" characterized the government's policies. [31] Tarriff legislation and surtaxes were among the instruments employed to "protect" the fledgling industries of Brazil. When the participation of the government was sought by manufacturers, the willingness of the patrimonial state to intervene in an area of new activity was evident.

With the increasing importance of industry in the Brazilian economy after World War I, the state moved into a position of influence and domination through protection and preemption of economic policy initiatives by private groups. As important, the impetus for industrialization often came from the old, traditional families or with their cooperation and forbearance. The result, as Fernando Henrique Cardoso tells us, is that the industrial bourgeoisie in Brazil has not developed a class consciousness that would facilitate group action; it remains a very heterogeneous group. There has been no need for a coordinated industrialist policy with regard to organized labor because the state carefully controls the working class. Because of the high level of profits in industry, supported by government favors and protection, industrialists "accept traditional practices and act more like groups linked to the old dominant classes than as a group that aspires to power." [32]

The only political action acceptable to the industrialists in Brazil is that which complements the policies of the state:

It consists of the personal participation in the game of compromises that patrimonial style politics, still dominant, offers to those that have resources to deal with the burden of clientelist politics. This participation

[31]Stanley J. Stein, *The Brazilian Cotton Manufacture* (Cambridge: Harvard University Press, 1957), p. 81.
[32]Fernando Henrique Cardoso, *Empresário Industrial e Desenvolvimento Econômico* (São Paulo: Difusão Européia do Livro, 1964), p. 161.

is highly rewarding for the industrialists, for by having access to the Congress and the President, they are able to gain economic advantages for their business groups without having to be concerned about any redefinition of the traditional political style. . . .[33]

And Warren Dean, in his study of industrialization in São Paulo, notes that after 1945 "the industrialists still shared most of the attitudes and interests of the planters, and when they did not, they were still willing to defer."[34] By the late 1950s and 1960s, "perhaps half of the industrial capital in São Paulo's private sector . . . was foreign-owned or controlled."[35] Dean concludes his analysis by stating that "the manufacturers were plainly disqualified from embarking their society upon a conscious policy of industrialization."[36] Domestic industry has gained the reputation of being of inferior quality; manufacturers bought local raw materials with reluctance, thus postponing the installation of basic industry. And the manufacturer, so dependent on the government for monopolies and special price-fixing and his penchant for political "deals," never gained a positive image among his fellow countrymen. "His success was not admired; nor did he embody the aspirations of the masses."[37]

An Economic Commission for Latin America analysis of postwar economic policies in Brazil indicated the preponderant role of the government in the economic realm:

Brazil's public sector owns . . . the country's maritime . . . rail transport facilities and its installations for the production of petroleum . . . controls most of the steelmaking sector, and is rapidly becoming the principal producer of electric energy. It . . . markets a considerable proportion of the exportable production; it is also the principal iron ore producer and exporter. It exercises direct . . . control over the exchange market . . . .

It constitutes . . . the major commercial banking enterprise since it accounts for about 35 percent of the general credit extended to the private sector through the *Banco do Brasil*, and most of the agricultural credit . . . Through other specialized financial agencies it grants the wages, interests rates, rents, and staple commodity prices. It sets minimum

[33]Ibid., p. 165.

[34]Warren Dean, *The Industrialization of São Paulo, 1880-1945* (Austin and London: University of Texas Press, 1969), p. 236.

[35]Ibid., p. 237.

[36]Ibid., p. 238.

[37]Ibid.

agricultural prices and is beginning to . . . operate a largescale storage and marketing system for agricultural commodities.

. . . It determines the composition of private investment and intervenes in the capital market.[38]

Leff comments that, given the political context of Brazilian economic development after World War II, "private sector industrialists were not able to stand in the way of the large expansion in the scope of the government's controls and regulation, or to curb its direct investment and production activities."[39]

In his study of representative associations in Brazil, Philippe Schmitter states that

the CNI (National Confederation of Industry) owes its prominence in good measure to its formal position as representative of industrialists in an industrializing economy, not to its actual performance in that position. Several respondents went out of the way to say that the CNI was "a facade organization" and to warn me not to pay too much heed to it.[40]

While the industrialists are not ignored, they are not central to economic decision-making. Their practical freedom is carefully circumscribed by state action. When a conflict arises between interest group aims and state policy, the latter will prevail. The industrialists of Brazil are not prepared for a showdown with the government, and with the increasing role played by the state there are indications that "the influence of industrialists' interest groups has even declined with industrialization."[41]

Thus we conclude that industrial groups have been no more successful than any other group in Brazilian society in challenging the growing hegemony of the patrimonial order. Late industrialization, a pattern of government intervention in economic policymaking and planning, a history of state paternalism, little industrial class solidarity, and a general cultural willingness to "leave it to the state" has inhibited the

[38]"Fifteen Years of Economic Policy in Brazil," *Economic Bulletin for Latin America,* Vol. 9 (November, 1964), 196-197, quoted in Leff, *Economic Policy-Making,* p. 35.

[39]Leff, *Economic Policy-Making,* p. 52.

[40]Schmitter, *Interest Conflict,* p. 320.

[41]Ibid., p. 361.

emergence of a strong, independent industrial sector. Since 1964 the increasing centralization of administrative and planning power in the hands of the central government and the state bureaucracy further limits the autonomy of the industrial groups. The heavy emphasis of the Military Republic on economic growth, as an indication of the "success" of the 1964 coup d'état, has meant that industrialists are a key group in the economic arena. While they have gained a great deal from the patronal sponsorship of the post-1964 governments in terms of support and protection, they have also sacrificed any hope of autonomous political action by their cooperation with the state. Short-term advantage has prevented the industrialists from reconsidering their role in Brazilian society.

THE LABOR MOVEMENT

The Brazilian labor movement has been described accurately in the following terms:

Labor relations with both the government and with employers evolved from a pattern of paternalism inherited from the colonial social structure which was dependent upon slavery. This has accounted for much worker apathy toward the labor union movement, making *personalismo* the basis of control of labor. In effect, the characteristics of the whole labor movement have often been a reflection of individual leaders, and until the late 1950s, attempts by labor union leaders or political parties to inspire a general class consciousness among workers received little popular support.[42]

The labor movement in general provides an excellent example of the co-option policy of the patrimonial state. Rather than allow the growth of an independent and perhaps destabilizing labor movement, each regime since 1930 has used its power to tie labor to the government, effectively precluding the creation of an autonomous, politically active interest group to represent workers' concerns.

A labor organization, the Labor Party (PT) organized in 1928, did not survive the Vargas coup in 1930. Vargas,

[42]U.S. Army, *Area Handbook for Brazil* (Washington: U.S. Government Printing Office, 1964), pp. 513-14.

identifying labor as a potential source of strength for his regime, quickly moved to co-opt the workers by providing them with benefits they had not requested. He interfered in labor organizational efforts and tied labor to the government legally and personally.

In November 1930 the Transitional Republic created the first ministry of labor by decree. Labor unions were legally recognized; new unions were stimulated. As a result of this new freedom, a number of strikes marred the early Vargas years. The 1934 Constitution then outlawed strikes and placed unions under police supervision. By 1937 any hint of an independent labor movement had disappeared.

The 1930-1937 period was one of mutual experimentation: to survive and flourish, the union leadership accepted government interference and direction; to assure social class conciliation and a dependent working class, the regime guaranteed union survival in exchange for its freedom. The concept of popular participation in labor policy never evolved in Brazil.

With the *Estado Novo* in 1937, a new labor policy was enunciated. Employers and workers were set up in parallel organizations. The basic units were the *sindicato* (union), the state federation, and three or more state federations joined in a confederation. One inclusive national labor organization was forbidden. This structure, which was never fully applied to employers, was imposed on the workers and survives today. Government recognition for all unions was required, while a series of labor courts replaced the concept of collective bargaining. Each worker needed a *carteira profissional* (identification card), issued by the government, to be employed. A union tax (*imposto sindical*) was required of all nonagricultural workers, employers, and the self-employed. For the worker the amount is one day's pay. Payments are made to the Bank of Brazil in the name of the worker's union. The tax money is distributed as follows: 60 percent for the union, 20 percent for the Union Social Fund, 5 percent to the confederation, and 15 percent to the federation. The tax funds are at the disposal of union leaders for education, welfare, and professional purposes as well as for a wide variety of political purposes.

In 1942 Vargas consolidated the paternalistic labor legislation, which remains the basic labor law of Brazil. It brought together the impressive welfare legislation of the Transitional Republic: a minimum wage, regulated working hours, improved health facilities, educational programs, and a carefully structured procedure for resolving conflicts with the employer.

In 1945 the Communist Party received government recognition; in the same year the PTB party was created. The communists soon returned to prominence in the labor federations and confederations. The PTB began to exercise its paternalistic control over labor through the labor ministry (a PTB member occupied that ministry for most of the years of the 1946 Republic) and the personal charisma of Vargas and the machinations of João Goulart. Not labor's party in terms of labor control, the PTB was nevertheless identified as such in the popular mind and worked diligently to hold that image.

The communist efforts led to the formation of the CTB-Confederation of Workers of Brazil during the early Dutra period. Both the CTB and the Communist Party were banned in 1947. Until Vargas returned to the presidency in 1951, trade unionism was severely curtailed. Although the 1946 Constitution incorporated the welfare legislation of the 1930s, workers' freedom was not acceptable under Dutra.

In the 1951-54 period, union elections were permitted, minimum wage levels were raised, and unions were allowed to affiliate with international labor organizations. The policy of nonharassment continued under Kubitschek (1956-61); more collective bargaining was allowed. With the advent of Goulart as president in 1961, labor moved into its period of greatest independence — ironically. As labor minister and PTB leader, Goulart had successfully posed as labor's advocate regardless of government policy. As head of the government he found himself pressured for inflationary wage increases, greater welfare legislation, strike protection, etc., all issues that would further weaken his administration if granted. Labor became more militant. The CGT — General Workers Command — an illegal entity formed to coordinate the confederations in the absence of a national organization, served as a goad for increased radicalism. By 1964 the confederations and the CGT were heavily influenced by the Communist Party.

The patrimonial system spawned a labor figure of interest, the *pelego,* a go-between or intermediary who builds his career on his ability to reconcile the often-conflicting interests of workers, employers, and government. The fee he receives for his work is justified in terms of the contribution he makes to the maintenance of good relations among the competing groups.

Schmitter's comments about the labor leaders of the early 1946 Republic are applicable to the decades following: "The syndical leadership of long standing, closely associated with the bureaucrats of the Labor Ministry and the Retirement and Social Welfare Institutes and loyal to the idea of a paternalist reformist state as the protector and benefactor of the labor movement, retained its hold on the top posts."[43] Whether the populist Vargas or the authoritarian Médici, labor continues to serve the interests of the state before its own.

With the March 31 movement, the CGT was abolished, unions were intervened, and close government supervision was reestablished. Communist leaders were purged. By 1966 most of the intervened unions had been "purified" and returned to dependable hands. The military regime's program of *novo trabalhismo* in 1966 and 1967 emphasized assistance to the unemployed and scholarships for the children of working families. A decree of September 8, 1967, said that the "unions of all kinds ought to be true schools of moral and civic education."[44] Speaking on May Day the minister of labor said in 1970 that "the unions will transform themselves, little by little, into new schools, new infirmaries of medical assistance, new residential and consumer cooperatives . . . " He continued to say that the president of the republic "is the number one worker of Brazil . . . " and that the ministry was the workers' "companion."[45]

As Table 16 indicates, more than 50 percent of Brazil's working population remained in agriculture in the 1960s (compared to 19.8 percent in Argentina and 31.5 percent in Chile). The area of greatest growth from 1920 to 1960 was the tertiary sector: 33.9 percent in 1960, an increase of about 100 percent since 1920. Thus labor legislation was aimed at the smallest sector, the secondary (12.2 percent in 1960). In terms of salaried employment (1950) only 33.7 percent in agricultural

[43]Schmitter, *Interest Conflict*, p. 129.
[44]Decree 61,314 of September 8, 1967.
[45]*Jornal do Brasil* (Rio), May 2, 1970.

Table 16
HISTORICAL EVOLUTION OF THE COMPOSITION OF LABOR FORCE

	Primary[a]	Percent Secondary[b]	Tertiary[c]
1920	70.5	13.0	16.5
1940	67.6	9.6[d]	22.9
1950	60.5	13.0[d]	26.5
1960	53.8	12.2[d]	33.9

[a]Primary = Agriculture and mining   [b]Secondary = Manufacturing and construction
[c]Tertiary = All other   [d]Includes electricity and utilities

Source: Joseph R. Ramos, *Labor and Development in Latin America* (New York: Columbia University Press, 1970), Table 15, p. 144. Reprinted by permission of the publisher.

were salaried; 87.1 percent in manufacturing, 51.4 percent in commerce, and 75.2 percent in services.[46] The change in the proportion of sectoral salaried employment in Brazil, from 1940 to 1950, indicated the lack of growth in agriculture: 0.2 percent in agriculture, 10.1 percent in manufacturing, 0.3 percent in commerce, and 4.1 percent in services. [47]

The labor legislation of the Transitional Republic was never extended to rural workers. Part of Vargas's compromise with the traditional rural oligarchy when he assumed power was that rural labor, the source of economic influence and social prestige for the rural elites, would not be politicized. The urban working class was fair game; the rural laborer was not. This tacit agreement continued in effect during the 1946 Republic's early years. By the mid-1950s, the policy of official neglect of the rural sector by the government was challenged hesitantly. By the early 1960s the rural sector, particularly in the Northeast, had become a source of radical agitation and political competition. The evolution of the rural union movement demonstrates a number of interesting aspects of the patrimonial order in Brazil.

The Rural Labor Movement

Early labor legislation specifically excluded rural workers,

[46]Joseph R. Ramos, *Labor and Development in Latin America* (New York and London: Columbia University Press, 1970), p. 113.
[47]Ibid., p. 116.

or the sections of the laws that extended legal protection to the countryside were never implemented. Not until March 2, 1963, did the congress pass the Rural Labor Statute, which provided a means of enforcing existing legislation for the benefit of rural laborers. Even before the congress acted, as part of the basic reform strategy of the Goulart government, the unionization effort in the Northeast had gained considerable momentum.

The first organized program of collective peasant action was that in Pernambuco, the Peasant Leagues (*Ligas Camponesas*), as they came to be called. Organized in 1955 by Francisco Julião, a state assemblyman and lawyer, son of a landowning family, they grew out of a mutual assistance burial association. When peasants asked Julião for legal help, he introduced a bill to have the state government expropriate three unused plantations for distribution to the workers. Julião became an immediate hero. *Ligas* spread quickly into neighboring states, with an estimated membership of 100,000, concentrated in the humid farming strip along the Northeastern coast called the *Zona da Mata*. Tenant farmers and sharecroppers were the major participants.

In the early 1960s competition for the support of the peasants emerged from within the Church. Bishops such as Dom Eugênio Sales (today a cardinal) moved to counter Julião and the growing communist influence on the peasants. Fathers Paulo Crespo and Antônio Melo in Pernambuco succeeded in organizing the first statewide Federation of Rural Workers in 1962. By April 1964, in one state of the Northeast,

more than 100 peasant associations (leagues and Catholic unions) existed in Pernambuco. Their combined membership was estimated to be about 280,000. Direct control of peasant organization was no longer solely in the hands of Julião or the Catholic Church. Between 1962 and 1964, representatives of the Brazilian Communist Party (PCB, the Moscow-oriented group), the Communist Party of Brazil (PC do B, influenced by the Chinese doctrinal position), the Leninist Vanguard (Trotskyite), the administration of the state's Governor, Miguel Arraes, and the administration of President João Goulart also, competed for the privilege of organizing Pernambucan peasants.[48]

[48]Cynthia N. Hewitt, "Brazil: The Peasant Movement of Pernambuco, 1961-1964," in Henry A. Landsberger (ed.), *Latin American Peasant Movements* (Ithaca and London: Cornell University Press, 1969), pp. 374-75.

Anthony Leeds has characterized Julião's leadership of the *Ligas* as in the typical paternalist mold of Brazil.[49] The same can be said of the Goulart administration's motives in moving into the rural union area. The rural labor movement was a movement from "on top" with the benefits handed down to the waiting peasants. Little peasant initiative appeared in any of the unionization efforts; the struggle was among competing national elite groups: the Church, university students from JUC and AP, the politicians, and the ideologues.

The First National Congress of Rural Workers and Laborers in Belo Horizonte in November 1961 was prophetic: it was divided by the competing groups who sought to use it for their own ends. By November 1963 and the the organization of CONTAG (National Confederation of Agricultural Workers), Julião had been elected to congress and was a marginal leader in the movement. A coalition of communists and radical Catholics defeated the more moderate church group for control of the confederation; the *Ligas* had not participated in the meeting.

By late 1963, then, there was a good deal of activity in the countryside. The protection of national labor legislation had been extended into the rural area for the first time. A number of competitive groups fought with each other to organize the peasants, under the new legal provisions, for their own political or institutional advantage. The issues of agrarian reform, the eradication of illiteracy, and the standardization of a living wage and just working conditions for rural workers produced an extraordinarily confusing convergence of diverse interests.[50] The resulting mobilization of the peasants terrified the rural oligarchy and raised the specter of massive internal disorder for the military. The presence of the communists and the obvious influence of Fidel Castro and his revolutionary message in the work of many of the groups convinced many military figures that the movement was subversive.

With the 1964 coup all subversive units were closed. The CONTAG, its federations and unions, were intervened by the

[49]Anthony Leeds, "Brazil and the Myth of Francisco Julião," in Joseph Maier and Richard W. Weatherhead (eds.), *Politics of Change in Latin America* (New York: Frederick A. Praeger, 1964), pp. 190-204.

[50]See Hewitt, "Brazil: The Peasant Movement of Pernambuco," for a discussion of these issues.

government. After a year of cleaning out the rural movement, the military regime has followed a policy of cautious corporatism and gradual paternalism in the countryside.[51] With the passage of an agrarian reform law in 1965 and the creation of a series of land reform institutes and agencies, the issue has become one of control and censorship by the government. The welfare legislation of the 1962-64 period will be applied to the rural workers, generally, but under the protection of the patrimonial regime and without popular participation. Rather than the radical agrarian reform called for at the National Congress of Rural Workers in 1961 and repeated by CONTAG in 1963-64, the government sponsors colonization projects in the Amazon and education and welfare programs. The small but real advances made in the countryside before 1964 were neutralized with the coup of March 31.

THE STATE BUREAUCRACY

The growth and influence of the federal bureaucracy and, perhaps as important, the reasons for its expansion are rooted in Brazilian political history. The expansion of the Portuguese empire necessitated a large administrative structure. With the Napoleonic wars and the removal of the royal court to Rio de Janeiro in 1808, public positions (*cargos públicos*) as sinecures became an accepted part of Brazilian administration.[52]

During the succeeding century the federal bureaucracy remained relatively small. The nation was overwhelmingly rural and agricultural, and the responsibilities of the national government concerned the few urban centers only. A highly diffuse network of state administrative systems grew up to serve the needs of the local political clans of the interior. During the period of the Old Republic "only two basic functions remained for the administrative system: the furnishing of employment for marginal members of the upper sector and the supplying of minimal services for the national government and for commercial interests involved in foreign trade."[53]

[51]Ibid.
[52]Lawrence S. Graham, *Civil Service Reform in Brazil: Principles versus Practice* (Austin and London: University of Texas Press, 1968), p. 17.
[53]Ibid., p. 22.

Under Vargas after 1930, with authority and control concentrated in the presidency, the bureaucracy expanded rapidly. In 1938 the Administrative Department of the Public Service (DASP) was created to serve the administrative system; it seldom, if ever, succeeded in sheltering the bureaucracy from the realm of patronage. Time and again efforts were made to create an elite career service, but the political needs of the executive always intervened. From 1945 to 1964, "despite the merit standards in Brazilian law, political patronage functioned as the predominant criterion in the selection of federal employees."[54]

The efforts of the national government since 1964 have aimed at controlling the proliferation of the bureaucracy in order to make it a more efficient instrument for economic modernization objectives. The group within the bureaucracy that has received the most attention is that of the *técnicos,* or technocratic planners, as opposed to the *burocratas,* or traditional administrators[55] (the corresponding terms used earlier were administrative and spoils sectors in the bureaucracy). The *técnicos* are development-oriented, concerned with reform and necessary structural modification; they are "scientific" in that their plans are elaborated after careful study and supposedly with little concern for politics, understood to mean, perjoratively, the old-style, pre-1964 politics. The *burocratas* are concerned with preserving the traditional political system and their positions in it. They execute the decisions made by others and do not see their role as a dynamic, innovative one. Octavio Ianni states that the *burocratas* function to maintain the status quo, while the *técnicos* are concerned with reform and change. In many societies, the role of the *técnicos* is one of both initiating and responding to new social and economic needs; in Brazil their role since 1964 has been limited to the narrower economic area.

Before 1964 the *técnicos,* while present in the federal bureaucracy, were outnumbered and their efforts vetoed by the political needs of the post-1945 regimes. After 1964 new men were introduced into the bureaucracy; a large number of the

---

[54]Ibid., p. 125.

[55]Octavio Ianni, *Estado e Capitalismo* (Rio de Janeiro: Editôra Civilização Brasileira, 1965), pp. 185-98.

spoils bureaucracy were dismissed; the ministries and agencies of the government were purged; and a major governmental reorganization allowed the *técnicos* free rein to plan the future economic transformation of the nation. Those *técnicos* who were considered to be politically "safe," such as Roberto Campos, were utilized by the military; others, such as Celso Furtado, lost their political rights and went into exile.[56]

The emphasis on central planning began after Vargas's fall from power in 1945. But only after 1964 have the technical and political aspects of planning coincided.[57] During the 1946 Republic lip-service was paid to the concept of planning – plans were elaborated, but they were vitiated by the practical political problems of the era. After 1964 the military were able to control the political system and, simultaneously, endorse the technical aspects of central planning as a means of legitimizing their rule through economic success.

Efforts by the Vargas regime in 1942 and 1943 to write five-year plans had little success. Two missions from the United States, one in 1942 and the other in 1943, assisted the Brazilian government in drawing up lists of investment priorities with limited effect on government policy. In 1946-47, the Dutra government prepared the SALTE Plan to coordinate existing plans but it was not approved by Congress until 1950: "while the idea of planning as a regular governmental function had gained much ground, the political and administrative will to insure implementation of planning was totally lacking."[58]

Some progress was made during Vargas's presidential term (1951-54) in utilizing the SALTE Plan, but a more important development was the contribution of the Joint Brazil–United States Technical Commission. Organized in 1948, it carried out its work from 1951 to 1953. Its principal task was to provide needed technical assistance for preparing loan applications for development projects to be submitted to international lending agencies and the United States. An important result of the work of the commission was the organization in 1952 of the National Bank for Economic Development (BNDE), which employed and

[56]See Leff, *Economic Policy-Making*, pp. 143-53, for a discussion of *técnicos*.
[57]Robert T. Daland, *Brazilian Planning: Development Politics and Administration* (Chapel Hill: University of North Carolina Press, 1967), p. 7.
[58]Ibid., p. 30.

trained many of the nation's *técnicos* during the succeeding decade and preserved the concept of rational, scientific planning. The work of the commission resulted in little else of substance; with the onset of the Eisenhower administration there were few public funds available for development support in Washington.

When he took office in 1956, President Kubitschek announced a program of thirty goals to be achieved by the end of his five-year term. He organized a Council of Development, a planning and advisory unit for the chief executive. The Program of Goals had a mixed record by 1961, but it had succeeded in focusing attention on planning throughout Kubitschek's term of office.

João Goulart's Three-Year Plan for Economic and Social Development, 1963-65 (*Plano Trienal*) was written under the direction of Celso Furtado, then serving as planning minister as well as superintendent of the Northeast Development Agency, SUDENE. Based on an impressive array of economic and social data, the plan contained a series of policy directives, "*guides* to planning rather than blueprints."[59] The plan failed because of the political use to which it was put by the Goulart government. As well, Brazilians tended to accept or reject the document in accordance with their own political beliefs: those who supported Goulart generally favored it; those opposing the president denounced the plan. Eventually even political supporters of the president criticized the document, and it was dropped after accomplishing some short-term political goals of the administration.

Although a number of regional development plans were drawn up between 1946 and 1964, the most prominent was that of the SUDENE, prepared by Celso Furtado and his staff. A five-year plan, to be updated annually, it was endorsed by the congress after a bitter debate and opposition from the traditional interests in 1959; it was funded only in 1961. The Master Plan for the Northeast emphasized infrastructural investment, but it also served to gather regional support for social and political change in the underdeveloped area. SUDENE lost its autonomy in 1964 and became part of the federal government's

[59]Ibid., p. 57.

overall planning effort.[60]

After the 1964 coup, Minister of Planning Roberto Campos (a former president of the BNDE and former Brazilian ambassador to the United States) masterminded the Program of Economic Action of the Government (PAEG) for 1964-66. The PAEG represented, for Campos and his fellow *técnicos,*

an essentially "technocratic" approach to the complex problems of economic policy. Their diagnosis did not differ radically from previous planning documents, even that of the Goulart government. The sharp contrast lay in the team's determination to follow through on their full implementation, confident that the President would extend his full backing rather than sacrifice financial stabilization measures in the face of the inevitable political protests from labor (over wage freezes) and producers (over credit restrictions).[61]

The PAEG was followed by the Strategic Program of the Costa e Silva government and, most recently, the Goals and Foundations for the Action of the Government of President Médici. Not a plan in the strict sense, the Médici government program builds on the efforts of the previous two administrations. The First National Plan of Economic and Social Development, 1971-73, to be revised annually, in accord with the directions of Complementary Acts 43 and 76 issued in 1969, is Médici's first coordinated planning document.

The *técnicos* are in firm control of Brazil's central planning efforts, and they have made inroads into the traditional or spoils bureaucracy. For the first time in Brazilian history the political power of the chief executive supports global planning as a means of furthering the country's development. But, thus far, the emphasis has been on economic growth almost exclusively. It remains to be seen if *técnico* planning will embrace the social issues that confront Brazil today now that ideas and resources have been made to coincide in the Military Republic.

[60]See Riordan Roett, *The Politics of Foreign Aid in the Brazilian Northeast* (Nashville: Vanderbilt University Press, 1972) for a discussion of Furtado, SUDENE, and the Northeast.

[61]Ronald M. Schneider, *The Political System of Brazil: Emergence of a "Modernizing" Authoritarian Regime, 1964-1970* (New York and London: Columbia University Press, 1971), pp. 150-51.

CONCLUSION

In this chapter we have seen the interplay of the patrimonial state with the Church, university students, industrialists, the labor movement, and the bureaucracy. In the period since 1964, the Church has chosen to emphasize its institutional survival rather than to confront the state over social issues. Students have been denied any public role in criticizing government policies; those who refuse to accept the regime's dictates are dealt with harshly. A small minority defect to the urban guerrilla movement to carry on what they feel to be a just struggle. The fledgling peasant movement has been co-opted by the patrimonial state much as urban labor served the populist needs of Getúlio Vargas; today the organized labor movement remains a dependency of the government. The industrialists, while benefiting from the economics of the regime, remain subservient to, and dependent on, the government. The federal bureaucracy, in the hands of the *técnicos,* now plays a central role in reenforcing the capabilities of the state in carrying out its development goals, narrowly defined in terms of economic growth.

The freedom of association, the pluralist model of political behavior, the ideal of popular participation in policy-making have had and will have little relevance for Brazil. Both historical tradition and contemporary power realities confirm the continuity and strength of the traditional order, made stronger by its determined effort to utilize the state bureaucracy to implement its goals efficiently.

6
The Military Republic, 1964 to the Present

Hélio Juguaribe has coined the phrase *Estado Castorial* (Sinecure State) to denote the process by which public power limits and co-opts independent action by social groups in Brazil.

The essence of this system consisted in a bargain whereby patronage was accorded in return for the promise of support. The state served to foster and protect the existing regime, and at the same time provided the necessary number of sinecures to insure the political support which the ruling class would otherwise have lacked, and which was needed in order to preserve its economic and political control of the country.[1]

He comments elsewhere that:

The ruling class indirectly subsidizes the idleness and marginality of the middle class by incorporating it within the *Estado Castorial,* and the middle class returns this tax by supporting clientelistic politics and the semicolonial and semifeudal (social) structure.[2]

A similar theme has been developed by Cândido Mendes.[3]

[1] Hélio Jaguaribe, "The Dynamics of Brazilian Nationalism," in Claudio Veliz (ed.), *Obstacles to Change in Latin America* (New York: Oxford University Press, 1965), p. 168.

[2] Hélio Jaguaribe, *Condicões Institucionais do desenvolvimento* (Rio de Janeiro: Instituto Superior de Estudos Brasileiros, 1958) quoted in Philippe C. Schmitter, *Interest Conflict and Political Change in Brazil* (Stanford: Stanford University Press, 1971), p. 282.

[3] Cândido Mendes de Almeida, "Sistema Político e Modelos do Poder no Brasil," *Dados,* No. 1 (second semester), 1966, pp. 7-41; and "Elite de Poder, Democracia, e Desenvolvimento," *Dados,* No. 6, 1969, pp. 57-90.

He identifies the emergence of new "power elites" in Brazilian politics since 1964, military in inspiration and compatible with the continued position of influence occupied by the traditional elites of the patrimonial state. The outstanding example of this new elite group is the technocratic administrator who occupies a central position in the decision-making apparatus of the Military Republic.

What these and other writers have pinpointed is the continuing power of the state.

Students of Brazilian society have suggested that the principal focus of the political struggle there has been to gain control over the administrative apparatus of the state. Once obtained, this control was not exercised as a means for molding or transforming the society according to the image of some cohesive social elite, nor was it exercised simply to provide that elite with immediate material or status rewards. It was used primarily as an instrument of political accommodation or conciliation for indirectly maintaining the status quo.[4]

In this chapter we will examine the 1964-71 period, that of the Military Republic. Our analysis will focus on the mechanisms developed by the armed forces to govern the patrimonial state. In chapter 5 we indicated the marginal position assigned nongovernmental groups in Brazil since 1964. This chapter will focus primarily on the centralization of power in the federal government and the impact on the political party system and the congress.

THE REVOLUTION DEFINES ITSELF: THE INSTITUTIONAL ACTS

There are many ways of dividing the period from 1964 to 1971. For purposes of both coherence and analysis, the divisions I will employ here are those that correspond to the most significant pronouncements of the March 31 movement: the Institutional Acts. The First Institutional Act appeared on April 9, 1964; the second on October 27, 1965; the fifth on December 13, 1968; and, carrying the same import as these

[4] Schmitter, *Interest Conflict*, p. 282.

Acts, Constitutional Amendment No. 1 of October 20, 1969. These are the most significant dates of the military regime that has ruled Brazil since the successful coup d'état of March 31, 1964.

The Institutional Acts are a significant and interesting departure in Brazilian political life. These documents constitute the justification for military intervention and also provide a political framework within which major institutional and structural reforms have been made. While not canceling the constitution, whether it be that of 1946 or 1967, the Acts supercede and restrict the purview of that document. In so doing, the principle of constitutional rule is brought into focus and the raison d'être of the movement of March 31 is better comprehended. The Acts represent the efforts of the armed forces to restore the influence of the patrimonial regime after 1964. As such, they represent a running commentary on the inadequacies of the 1946 Republic, as well as formal notification to the nation that the changes introduced in 1964 are considered permanent.

It seems clear that the military feel the need to preserve the myth of constitutionalism that has marked Brazilian history in both the nineteenth and the twentieth centuries. It is also clear that the military regime feels little compunction in violating both the spirit and the letter of the constitution when it is deemed necessary in the interests of the Revolution. Thus, the Institutional Acts represent the reality of the 1964 movement in that they are the authoritative statements of the regime's political purpose; the constitution remains a legal exercise that is retained because it signifies so little in reality. It is a juridical statement of intent, not a political document of relevance to the governance of the Brazilian state.

Seventeen Institutional Acts and seventy-seven Complementary Acts were issued between 1964 and the end of 1969. The Complementary Acts spelled out the specific intent of the more general principle involved in the Institutional Acts. It is clear from the wording of the Acts that they have been decreed by the armed forces acting in a dual role: that of the representatives of the movement of March 31, the Revolution, which has a life of its own apart from any institutional or constitutional restraints and as the executive power of the

Brazilian government. The dividing line between the armed forces and the government is at best tenuous; in the area of major legal and juridical innovation it is even more hazy.

The 1967 Constitution emerged, in part, from a feeling that the changes brought about by the early Institutional Acts and the Complementary Acts required incorporation into the constitution and that the 1946 document no longer served the needs of the nation. With the First Constitutional Amendment of October 1969, it became clear that the 1967 Constitution was an impermanent statement to be ignored when required by the interests of the armed forces in their efforts to restore the status quo to Brazil.

The First Institutional Act

The presidency of Brazil was declared vacant on the night of April 1, 1964, by the president of the senate. The president of the chamber of deputies was sworn in as acting president early on April 2. The nation — and the civilian political elite — waited.

After a week of negotiation over the course of the March 31 coup, the armed forces decided to act unilaterally. The political initiative passed to the military; it remained in their hands throughout the remainder of the sixties. On April 9 the three military ministers issued an Institutional Act; it would become known as the First Institutional Act when others appeared. The Act did not rest on any constitutional justification; its authority derived from the moral force of the Revolution itself. No further justification was deemed necessary.

The preamble of the Act states the reason for its issuance:

The successful revolution invests itself with the exercise of the Constitutent Power, which manifests itself by popular election or by revolution. This is the most expressive and radical form of the Constitutent Power. Thus, the successful revolution, like the Constitutent Power, is legitimized by itself. The Revolution dismisses the former government and is qualified to set up a new one. The Revolution holds in itself the normative strength inherent to the Constitutent Power, and establishes judicial norms without being limited by previous norms.

The Act vastly strengthened the powers of the chief executive. While the 1946 Constitution remained in force, it was subject to modification by the Act. The president received the power to propose amendments to the constitution which the congress had to consider within thirty days; only a majority vote, as opposed to the 2/3 vote stipulated in the 1946 Constitution, was needed for approval. Only the president could submit expenditure measures to congress, and the congress could not increase the amount stipulated in the bills. The power to declare a state of siege without congressional approval was given to the president, and the executive was granted the power to suppress the political rights of "political undesirables" for a period of ten years.

The Act decreed that the election of the new president, to replace Goulart, and the vice-president would be by an absolute majority of the congress, to take place within two days of the promulgation of the Act. The date for the election of the next president and vice-president, to assume office on January 31, 1966, was set for October 3, 1965. On April 11, 1964, General Humberto Castello Branco, a leader of the March 31 coup, was elected president.

Article X of the Act, which gave the president the right to revoke legislative mandates and to suspend political rights, was to expire on June 15, 1964. The military government moved quickly to revoke the mandates of those members of congress identified with the defeated left. By the deadline, three former presidents — Kubitschek, Quadros, and Goulart — as well as six governors and more than forty members of congress, plus some three hundred individuals active in political life, had had their rights suspended. Under Article VII, which gave the president the power to expel people from the civil service without regard for existing legislation guaranteeing employment, it is estimated that approximately 9,000 people were fired by November 9, the cutoff date stated in the Act.

As the military became accustomed to their new political role, it was clear to them that they would not finish their task by January 20, 1966, the date on which the presidential term of Castello Branco would terminate. In July 1964, therefore, a constitutional amendment extended the president's term of office until March 15, 1967; new presidential elections were set for November 1966.

With the decision to extend the president's term, implying a military commitment to retain power for an indefinite period, a number of events in 1965 helped to determine the political strategy of the regime. The first was the election, in the mayoralty race in São Paulo in March 1965, of a candidate backed by former President Quadros. The victory of a man identified by some as a representative of the populist tradition in Brazilian politics (even though a military officer), provided the impetus required for a move away from the economic emphasis of the Revolution into the political arena.

On July 15, 1965, two laws dealing with elections and political parties were announced. These represented the first substantive revision of the pre-1964 political rules of the game. The Electoral Code reduced the number of parties by increasing the minimum requirement that parties had to meet to achieve or maintain legal status. Electoral alliances were forbidden; candidates were required to reside in the area they sought to represent; voters were required to choose legislators from the same party in order to strengthen party discipline; and the running mates of successful gubernatorial and presidential candidates were automatically elected. These reforms were an attempt to deal with one of the problems perceived by the military as most debilitating in the pre-1964 era: the weak and diffuse multiparty system. It was hoped that these reforms would introduce some coherence into the political system.

The Political Party Statute stipulated stringent procedures for the organization of new political parties. Individuals were forbidden to run for more than one office in any election. Residence and party membership requirements were specified for candidates. It was hoped, with this law, to control the problem of representation, so abused before 1964, when there were few requirements linking a candidate to his constituency.

Also promulgated on July 15 was an Ineligibilities Law. It prevented former ministers in the Goulart government (those appointed after the January 1963 plebiscite) from candidacy. Its primary purpose was to prevent the candidacy of several prominent anti-regime politicians in the upcoming state elections.

Although all three proposals were submitted to congress for consideration, two became law without final action by that body. When the time period for consideration expired, the president, using the authority granted to him by the Institutional Act, acted unilaterally. The Political Party Statute was passed by the congress, but fourteen items introduced during floor debate were vetoed by the president. It appeared in the form in which it was originally submitted to the congress.

The gubernatorial elections of October 1965 were a critical event in the unfolding of the military regime. Over the warning and the fears of many members of the armed forces, the Castello Branco government determined to hold open, competitive elections. Two candidates identified as opponents of the regime (Israel Pinheiro in Minas Gerais and Negrão de Lima in Guanabara), both supported by former President Kubitschek, were victorious.

Immediately the military hard liners pressed the government to annul the elections. In order to fulfill his promise to allow the inauguration of all candidates elected, President Castello Branco promulgated a Second Institutional Act.

The Second Institutional Act — October 27, 1965

The October 1965 elections, in retrospect, were a crucial event in determining the unfolding of the movement of March 31. Before the results were known, it was assumed that direct elections would continue to be the method employed to select new members of the political government elite. With the publication of the Second Act, the military regime made a basic decision to restructure national politics to try to insure that the legacy of the 1946 Republic would be effectively neutralized. The elections seem to have been the determining factor in the decision of Castello Branco and the moderate wing of the military that the unity of the armed forces was more important for the future development of Brazil than was the constitutional principle of direct elections.

The Second Act determined that only the president could create new positions in the civil service; further restricted the time allowed to congress to consider legislation before it became law automatically; increased the number of members of the Supreme Court (the court had been viewed as a last holdout against the more blatantly unconstitutional actions of the Revolutionary government); reserved the right of nomination of all federal judges to the president of the republic; reorganized the Supreme Military Tribunal; stipulated that civilians accused of crimes against national security were to be submitted to military justice; decreed the indirect election of the president and the vice-president by an absolute majority of the federal congress; permitted the president to declare a state of siege for 180 days to prevent "the subversion of internal order"; extended the right of the Revolution to suspend individual political rights for ten years; established restrictions on the activities of those whose political rights were removed; gave the president the right to intervene in the states of the federation, in addition to the reasons stipulated in the Constitution, in order to assure the execution of a federal law and in order to prevent or punish the subversion of order; abolished the existing political parties and canceled their registration; excluded from judicial competence all acts of the Supreme Revolutionary Command and by the federal government in the First and Second Acts and in the Complementary Acts to follow, plus resolutions passed since March 31, 1964, of assemblies canceling the mandates of legislators; and giving the president the power to recess congress, legislative assemblies, and chambers of municipal counselors. The Second Act's jurisdiction was to continue until March 15, 1967, the date of the inauguration of Castello Branco's successor.

The political party situation was further modified by Complementary Act No. 4 of November 20, 1965, which provided for the provisional registration of political organizations sponsored by at least 120 federal deputies and 20 senators. Two parties emerged, replacing the fourteen-party system of the 1946 Republic; a government-sponsored entity, the National Renovating Alliance (ARENA), and the opposition group, the Brazilian Democratic Movement (MDB). ARENA became a UDN stronghold with some PSD support. MDB attracted the remains of the PTB and some PSD elements.

Another Institutional Act, the Third, issued on February 5, 1966, replaced direct election of governors with selection by state legislatures on September 3, 1966, scheduled legislative elections for federal senators and deputies and state deputies for November 15, 1966, and eliminated the election of mayors of major capital cities. They would, henceforth, be selected by the governors of the states.

The Complementary Acts announced through 1965 and 1966 served to implement or elaborate the Institutional Acts. Perhaps the most notorious Complementary Act promulgated during this time was the 23rd, of October 20, 1966; it confirmed the growing centralization of power in the hands of the military and strengthened the determination of the government to allow little, if any, organized opposition to its plans. It was preceded by the cassation of six federal deputies on October 12 and a break with the government by the ARENA congressional leadership. The 23rd Complementary Act decreed the recess of the federal congress until November 22, 1966 – after the scheduled elections. The Act stated that there existed in the congress "a group of counterrevolutionary elements whose objective was to disturb the public peace and upset the coming election of November 15, thus compromising the prestige and the authority of the legislative power . . ." A precedent had been established, allowing the executive power to quiet the legislative branch successfully whenever it suited the government's needs.

Throughout 1966 the administration worked to assure that candidates acceptable to the Revolution would be chosen by the new political parties. It would allow no repetition of the 1965 nominating process. A series of Complementary Acts further strengthened the government's position vis-à-vis the political parties. Complementary Act No. 20 of July 19, 1966, for example, made it possible for an ARENA legislator to switch to, or vote for, the MDB candidate in either the presidential or gubernatorial elections.

With the indirect election by the national congress of Marshal Costa e Silva to succeed Castello Branco, the succession issue was settled. Costa e Silva ran unopposed; attempts by the MDB to launch a rival candidacy had failed. Direct elections on November 15 selected federal senators and deputies, state deputies, mayors and municipal councilmen. The ARENA party won overwhelmingly. ARENA elected senators from fifteen states and approximately two-thirds of the new deputies. (See Table 17 for a comparison of the congress in 1965, 1966, and 1970.)

The Fourth Institutional Act of December 7, 1966, convoked an extraordinary meeting of congress to vote and promulgate a new constitution. The preamble of the Fourth Act stated that it had become necessary to give the country a new constitution that would "represent the institutionalization of

Table 17
PARTY COMPOSITION OF CONGRESS IN THE MILITARY REPUBLIC

1965*			
Party	Senators	Deputies	Total
PSD	22	119	141
PTB	17	119	136
UDN	15	95	110
PSP	2	21	23
PDC	1	18	19
PTN	2	12	14
PR	1	5	6
PL	2	3	5
PRP	0	5	5
PST	0	4	4
MRT	1	3	4
PSB	1	2	3
PRT	0	3	3
Independents	2	0	2
TOTALS	66	409	475

*Elected in October 1962

1966			
ARENA	43	254	297
MDB	21	150	171
Independents	2	5	7
TOTALS	66	409	475

1970			
ARENA	59	223	282
MDB	7	87	94
TOTALS	66*	310**	376

*46 senators elected in November 1970   **172 deputies elected for the first time

Source: Revista Brasileira de Estudos Políticos, Nos. 23/24 (July 1967/January 1968), p. 9; Veja; and Jornal do Brasil.

the ideas and principles of the Revolution." The constitution was promulgated on January 24, 1967. It further strengthened the executive power and weakened any hope of opposition groups' using the constitution to justify opposition to the regime.

THE COSTA E SILVA GOVERNMENT

The Failure of the Opposition to Unite

With the inauguration of President Costa e Silva on March 15, 1967, the Revolution entered a new phase. The early and successful efforts at controlling inflation seemed to be working; the needed structural reforms of the political system had been undertaken; and the crises of confidence within the military seemed to have been overcome with the acceptance by Castello Branco of the Costa e Silva candidacy. The main political event of the first year of the second military government was the discussion about the formation of a united front of opposition forces.

The only significant attempt to organize a united political front against the military regime occurred between 1966 and 1968. Governor Carlos Lacerda of Guanabara, who saw his presidential ambitions destroyed by the military, assumed his traditional role in Brazilian politics and took the offensive against the regime. When former Presidents Kubitschek and Goulart were contacted, they evinced some interest in a united opposition movement.

In September, Lacerda met with Goulart in Montevideo and signed a pact with his former political enemy to proceed with the organization of the front. Upon his return, the executive committee of the MDB announced that it would not support the front; President Jânio Quadros let it be known that he would not join the movement. The ex-president of the PTB, Lutero Vargas, attacked the idea in October. And in a speech that received widespread publicity, Interior Minister Albuquerque Lima condemned the front as an attempt to take Brazil back to the days before 1964.

By early 1968 the movement to form a united opposition

front appeared badly fragmented. By the end of 1968 Lacerda had his political rights canceled, and the moving force behind the front collapsed into silence. The movement was declared illegal; moreover, members of congress supporting it were expelled from the congress and banned from political activity for ten years.

The front failed because of the suspicions among the potential leaders over the ambitions of Lacerda. Three former presidents and a principal presidential aspirant would find it difficult under any circumstances to form a united front. With the military regime expressing public disapproval and the political parties unwilling to cooperate, the chances of success among the political elite were slim if not nonexistent. The front aroused little popular interest; it did not provide a focus for dramatic civilian protest. It ended where it began — in the ambition of Carlos Lacerda to retain a prominent voice in national political affairs. The military in December 1968 effectively neutralized that ambition for at least a decade.

The Crisis of December 1968

Throughout the last half of 1968 it became apparent that the division within the regime had deepened between those who supported a moderate, semiconstitutional policy favoring limited civilian participation and the hard-line nationalists who argued for military preeminence in all matters. The president seemed to favor a more moderate line; the leading proponent of a rigorous, nationalist development policy, carried out by the military, was the interior minister, General Alfonso Albuquerque Lima.

Albuquerque Lima had a large following among the younger members of the officer corps. He believed in the necessity of prolonged military rule in order to modernize Brazil, a task the civilian politicians of the 1946 to 1964 period had failed miserably in achieving. For him, modernization meant structural reform of things such as the land-tenure system, the development and integration of the Amazon, the necessity of reducing regional imbalance, etc. The general believed that a great nation like Brazil could no longer ignore its underdeveloped regions; such a policy of neglect threatened national security and modernization.

The two positions were brought into confrontation over the issue of a speech made on the floor of the congress by deputy Márcio Moreira Alves. He urged Brazilians to boycott military parades on Independence Day and asked that parents not allow their daughters to date military personnel. The nationalists found this address disgraceful and expected that the government would take appropriate action against the deputy. President Costa e Silva attempted to utilize legal channels to convince the congress to remove Alves's congressional immunity, but the congress balked.

In late October a group of captains of the First Army stationed in Rio de Janeiro issued a manifesto. The document took note of their sacrifices for the Revolution, including their state of near-poverty amidst the plenty enjoyed by some. The message was unmistakable – the government was not responding to the basic needs of the nation. The modernization of the country required firm and decisive leadership; abusive and insolent disregard for national priorities from civilians was not to be tolerated.

On December 12, 1968, the congress met to consider the insistent request of the government that it lift Alves's immunity. Two hundred and sixteen members of congress voted against, 141 in favor, and 12 cast blank ballots. The government's demand had been rejected. In the face of this blatant disrespect for military authority, the government moved quickly to regain control of a rapidly deteriorating situation.

The Fifth Institutional Act – December 13, 1968

The Fifth Act stated that the "revolutionary process unfolding could not be detained." The very institutions given to the nation by the Revolution for its defense were being used to destroy it, said the preamble of the Act. The Fifth Act empowered the president to recess the national congress, legislative assemblies, and municipal councils by Complementary Acts. These bodies would again convene only when called by the president. In addition, the president could decree intervention in the states when in the national interests and without regard for the constitutional restrictions on intervention; he could suspend political rights of any citizen for ten years and cancel elected mandates without regard for constitutional limitations. The national state of siege was prolonged; the confiscation of personal goods illicitly gained was allowed; the right of habeas corpus was suspended in cases of political crimes, crimes against national security, and the social and economic order; and the restrictions to be placed on those who lost their political rights were increased and more explicitly designated.

Complementary Act No. 38, of December 13, 1968, decreed the recess of congress. With the closing of the legislature, the regime had determined the immediate future of the Revolution of March 31, 1964. It would be a period of outright military rule without the inconvenience of elected, civilian interference. The economic planning process, which represented the only significant accomplishment of the regime, would continue unfettered. The possibilities for "humanizing" the Revolution gave way to the necessity of internal security, that is, precluding overt opposition from civilian political groups, and development, to be determined by the military regime and its civilian supporters.

The issuance of the Act seemed to secure the leadership of the president within the regime. The governing coalition rallied behind the president. Albuquerque Lima's abrupt departure in January 1969 indicated that the government felt sufficiently in control to need his symbolic presence in the cabinet no longer.

The first eight months of 1969 saw a flurry of Revolutionary legislation. The Sixth Institutional Act (February 1, 1969) amended the 1967 Constitution (Article 113) and stipulated that the Supreme Court would consist of eleven members nominated by the president. It also said that the Superior Military Court would be responsible for trying all those accused of national security crimes.

The Seventh Institutional Act (February 26, 1969) regulated the functioning of legislative assemblies and municipal councils. It suspended interim elections for executive and legislative positions and decreed government intervention in case of vacancies. The president was empowered to set a new date for elections when he felt it to be useful.

Administrative reform of the states and municipalities, to conform to the model of the federal government, was decreed by the Eighth Institutional Act (April 2, 1969). A constitutional amendment facilitating government expropriation of, and compensation for, rural lands constituted the Ninth Institutional Act (April 26, 1969). The Tenth Act (May 18, 1969), further elaborated on the penalties that accompanied the suspension of political rights or the cancellation of elective office.

The Eleventh Institutional Act (August 14, 1969) established dates for the election of municipal officials which had been held in abeyance since the Seventh Act.

All of the Institutional Acts confirmed the assumption of supreme legislative power by the military regime. The military have felt secure in the exercise of the executive powers of government since March 1964, along with the closing of congress in December 1968 and the consequent amendments to the constitution. The Acts, and the promulgation of political decisions by means of the Acts, have affirmed the willingness of the regime to pursue its twin themes of security and development.

The President Incapacitated

Two dramatic events in August and September of 1969 demonstrated both the potential vulnerability and the military predominance in the 1964 regime: the incapacitation of President Costa e Silva and the kidnapping of U.S. Ambassador C. Burke Elbrick in Rio de Janeiro.

A massive stroke incapacitated President Costa e Silva in late August. By the 1967 Constitution, Vice-President Pedro Aleixo, a civilian from Minas Gerais, an old-line member of the defunct UDN, was next in succession. It was clear that the armed forces would determine if the constitutional succession would be observed. Within forty-eight hours of the president's illness, the Twelfth Institutional Act (August 31, 1969) was issued. The military had decided against the constitution. The ministers of the navy, the army, and the air force "in the name of the President of the Republic . . . temporarily impeded from exercising his functions for reasons of health" promulgated the Act. The document stated that:

> The situation that the country is experiencing . . . precludes the transfer of the responsibilities of supreme authority and supreme command of the Armed Forces, exercised by his excellency, to other officials, in accordance with the constitutional provision.
>
> As an imperative of National Security, it falls to the ministers of the Navy, of the Army and of the Air Force to assume, for as long as the head of the Nation is incapacitated, the duties given to his excellency by the constitutional documents in force.
>
> The Nation can have confidence in the patriotism of its military chiefs who, in this hour, as always, will know how to honor the historic legacy of their predecessors, loyal to the spirit of nationalism, the Christian formation of its people, contrary to extremist ideologies and violent solutions, in moments of political or institutional crises.

The Act, relatively short in length, stipulated that the military ministers would act on behalf of the president; that the previously published Institutional and Complementary Acts would remain in full force; and that all the acts and decisions of the government taken as a result of the Twelfth Act and its Complementary Acts would be beyond judicial purview.

The new Act demonstrated the willingness of the armed forces to violate the constitution they themselves had promulgated in 1967. No mention was made of the vice-president; none was required, really. It was clear that the ministers represented the general will of the military in assuming supreme command of the nation.

The American Ambassador Disappears

On Thursday, September 4, 1969, Ambassador Elbrick was taken at gunpoint from his limousine in Rio de Janeiro. A note from his kidnappers identified themselves as members of revolutionary movements; it demanded the release of fifteen political prisoners held by the regime in exchange for the life of the ambassador. A note found in the ambassador's car, addressed "to the Brazilian people," stated:

> With the kidnapping of the Ambassador we want to demonstrate that it is possible to defeat the dictatorship and the exploitation if we arm and

organize ourselves. We show up where the enemy least expects us and we disappear immediately, tearing out the dictatorship, bringing terror and fear to the exploiters, the hope and certainty of victory to the midst of the exploited.

The demands of the kidnappers were that their manifesto be published and that the fifteen prisoners be taken to Algeria, Chile, or Mexico, where they would be granted political asylum. A time limit of forty-eight hours was stated. The manifesto ended with a warning to the regime from the terrorists: "Now it is an eye for an eye, and a tooth for a tooth."

The government, in the hands of the military ministers, responded immediately. The fifteen political prisoners were rounded up from their places of detention and placed aboard a plane for Mexico; the manifesto appeared in the Brazilian newspapers. The list of prisoners included some of the leading critics and opponents of the regime. Amidst rumors that members of the officer corps were "unhappy" over the government's decision, the Thirteenth Institutional Act (September 5, 1969) appeared. It empowered the executive to banish from the national territory any Brazilian considered dangerous to national security.

The Fourteenth Institutional Act, issued the same day, stated: "Considering that acts of adverse psychological warfare and revolutionary or subversive war, that disturb the life of the country and maintain it in a climate of intranquility and agitation, deserve more severe repression...." The Act amended the constitution (Article 150) and established the penalties of death, perpetual imprisonment, banishment or confiscation of goods for those guilty of participating in psychological, revolutionary, or subversive war against the state.

THE URBAN GUERRILLA MOVEMENT IN BRAZIL

Previously deemphasized by the regime, the kidnapping of the American ambassador dramatically publicized the existence of a network of guerrilla bands operating in the cities of Brazil. This movement posed a most serious threat to the stability of the regime during the 1967-69 period. By challenging the authority of the government, the terrorist groups hoped to weaken the support for the military from the middle and upper urban sectors. If the government could not secure public order, what else justified its continuation? The terrorists had begun to have a real impact on the public mind with a series of daring bank robberies — more than a hundred by the end of 1969 — and public bombings.

The "official" opening of the terrorist war against the government began in early 1967. A bombing attempt aimed at then Minister of War Costa e Silva in the airport at Recife in March was the first evidence of a planned and organized guerrilla opposition. Other bombings and bank robberies followed. The kidnapping of the ambassador in September 1969 was a new plateau both in audacity and in challenge to the regime.

The terrorist groups stemmed from dissident elements of the Moscow-oriented Communist Party of Brazil (PCB) led for decades by Luís Carlos Prestes. The first breakoff had been with the formation of the Revolutionary Communist Party of Brazil (PCBR) with a decidedly Maoist or Fidelista orientation. Other fragments represented Trotskyite and Marxist variants.

The most prominent of the groups was the National Liberating Alliance (ALN) founded early in 1967, led by former Communist Party deputy Carlos Marighella. Committed to terrorist and guerrilla warfare, Marighella became the mastermind of the movement; the ALN combined within its ranks a number of smaller terrorist bands who looked to Marighella for leadership and ideological inspiration.

A group that worked closely with the ALN but maintained its own identity was that led by ex-Captain Carlos Lamarca. Called the Popular Revolutionary Vanguard (VPR), it merged with another group called the National Liberation Command (Colina) in June-July 1969 to form the Armed Revolutionary Vanguard (VAR), referred to as VAR-Palmares. Palmares was the site of an unsuccessful slave revolt in the late nineteenth century in the Brazilian Northeast. The VPR, in turn, had resulted from a fusion of other fragment terrorist groups. Under Lamarca's daring leadership, the VAR-Palmares became a romantic symbol of protest against the regime and attracted many students to its ranks. Disillusioned by military rule, they accepted Lamarca's leadership in, and Marighella's ideological justification for, armed insurrection. A pamphlet entitled *The Mini-Manual of the Urban Guerrilla* by Carlos Marighella, which appeared in the middle of 1969, offered a sophisticated and incisive summary of the bankruptness of the regime and the necessity of undermining it by urban revolutionary warfare.

The movement was not a monolithic entity. It was splintered and represented antagonistic views of Brazilian society, ranging from reformist to revolutionary/anarchistic. A Congress of VAR-Palmares, held in September 1969 to debate the future of the organization, resulted in further fragmentation of that group. The murder of Marighella in São Paulo in November 1969 weakened the revolutionary left considerably. The loss of Marighella and the continuing fragmentation of the radical left was accompanied by increasing effectiveness on the part of the regime. In the state of Guanabara, the Center of Operations of Internal Defense (CODI) brought together all the civilian police and armed forces units working on security. A similar movement in São Paulo, Operation Bandeirante (OBAN) united all federal and state police units. OBAN was successful in uncovering clandestine groups of many of the terrorist organizations and by the end of 1969 had made more than four hundred arrests.

The terrorist groups scored heavy blows against the regime during the first six months of 1970. A Japanese Consul in São Paulo and the West German ambassador in Rio de Janeiro were kidnapped and held hostage until the regime agreed to the release of political prisoners. Both groups of prisoners were flown into exile. An attempted kidnapping of the United States consul general in Porto Alegre was foiled by his personal bravery. The Swiss ambassador was kidnapped in December 1970 and released in exchange for prisoners.

But by 1972 it seemed that this challenge to the regime had been counteracted effectively. The terrorist groups had not weakened the regime in the eyes of its strongest supporters, the middle and upper sectors. On the contrary, these groups interpreted the guerrilla movement as added justification for strong and effective government. The promptness and humaneness with which the government dealt with the kidnappings of foreign diplomats (in contrast with the Guatemalan government, which had refused to negotiate with similar terrorists who then murdered the West German ambassador to Guatemala) reassured the international community that the regime was willing and able to release political prisoners without severely undermining its internal support. The death of Carlos Lamarca in a gun battle with security police in September 1971 deprived the guerrillas of their principal leader.

One of the most disturbing aspects of the campaign against the terrorists was the reported widespread use of torture by civilian and military authorities. Although the regime declared on numerous occasions that the allegations of torture were exaggerated, sufficient evidence emerged to substantiate the charge. The subject became an internal political issue in 1968 and 1969 as international press coverage dramatically exposed cases of torture. What had been employed originally as a tactic of repression against known guerrillas had been clearly extended to "political" prisoners not charged with terrorism. By the end of 1971, President Médici seemed convinced that the tortures had to be stopped. The question was whether or not his order would be followed by local and regional civilian and military police units. They justified their tactics in terms of internal security and the need to uproot the serious threat to political order posed by the guerillas.

CONSTITUTIONAL AMENDMENT NO. 1 — OCTOBER 20, 1969

As the regime surmounted the challenge to its authority that the kidnapping of the American ambassador represented, it became clear that the president's incapacitation was permanent. The country confronted the task of selecting its fifth chief executive in the 1960s.

The immediate issue concerned the constitutional succession — would Vice-President Aleixo be allowed to assume the presidency? The answer of the armed forces emerged on October 14, 1969, with the announcement of the Sixteenth Institutional Act. The high command of the armed forces, that is, the three service chiefs, promulgated the document:

... considering that the superior interests of the country require the immediate and permanent filling of the office of President of the

Republic; . . . considering that Institutional Act No. 12 (of August 31, 1969) . . . attributes to the military ministers the right to substitute for the President of the Republic in his temporary incapacitation . . . . Article 1. The position of President of the Republic is declared vacant . . . . Article 2. The position of Vice-President of the Republic is also declared vacant. . . .

By using an Institutional Act, with congress in recess, the prerogatives of that body were exercised by the executive power. By precluding the constitutional succession of the civilian vice-president, the military prepared the way for the creation of a more rigidly authoritarian government to succeed Costa e Silva.

The internal dynamics of the selection process for the new chief magistrate are not fully known.[5] It is commonly accepted that the officer corps of the three services was polled. At the time there were approximately 118 army generals, 60 admirals, and 61 air force brigadiers. These, plus other command officers (an estimated total of about 13,000 men), were asked to nominate those men thought most qualified to replace Costa e Silva. General Emílio Garrastazu Médici, a supporter of the stricken president and commander of the Third Army located in the state of Rio Grande do Sul, ranked highest. He was followed in popularity by General Orlando Geisel and General Alfonso Albuquerque Lima, the former interior minister. It is reliably reported that Albuquerque Lima had prepared a program of action which he discussed with the officer corps on trips to the various command posts before the final selection was made by the high command of the armed forces. In the end, General Médici, who is reported to have polled the most votes in all four armies, received the military nomination for the presidency. Admiral Augusto Hamman Rademaker Grunswald, then serving as navy minister, received the vice-presidential nomination.

The Sixteenth Act stipulated that the elections for president and vice-president would be held by the congress on October 25, 1969; those elected would take office on October 30; their term of office would terminate on March 25, 1974. The Act also clearly reserved the right of legislation to the

---

[5] For a detailed summary of the events surrounding the succession, see Ronald M. Schneider, *The Political System of Brazil: Emergence of a "Modernizing" Authoritarian Regime, 1964-1970* (New York and London: Columbia University Press, 1971), pp. 297-311.

military ministers even though the congress had been convened.

The political parties were given the right to nominate candidates for the offices. ARENA nominated Médici and Rademaker; the MDB did not offer nominations. The candidates of the Revolution were solemnly elected to the vacant positions by the congress on the 25th of October, 1969.

The Seventeenth Institutional Act of October 14, 1969, gave the president the power to transfer to the reserve any military officer guilty of violating the cohesion of the armed forces. The preamble of the Act stated that "the Armed Forces as institutions that serve to sustain the constituted powers of law and order, are organized on a basis of the principles of hierarchy and discipline. . . ." The Act can be interpreted as a warning to those officers in disagreement with the decision of the military high command in passing over Albuquerque Lima in favor of Médici. Also, the Act gave to the new president "legal" means of imposing the military's will on the armed forces without having to resort to other forms of coercion or intimidation.

The Sixteenth and Seventeenth Acts were followed by another unilateral decision of the military commanders: Constitutional Amendment No. 1 of October 17, published in the Official Diary on October 20 and in effect as of October 30. The effect of the Amendment has led some political observers to refer to the Amendment as the 1969 Constitution, even though 95 percent of the 1967 document remains. The Amendment, among other changes, reduced still further the powers of the congress; the size of the congress was reduced when the criterion for the number of seats was shifted from population (benefiting the more backward states with a large illiterate population) to registered voters (which benefits the more urban states in the South) — the new chamber of deputies was reduced from 409 to 293; the state assemblies were reduced from 1,076 to 672 seats; the centralized control of the chief executive over the introduction of new legislation, especially money bills, was confirmed.

The Amendment represented the determination of the military to insure a presidential succession unmarred by dissent or protest. It provided the new chief executive with all the powers required for governing and controlling the nation. By moving to promulgate these decisions before the election of General Médici, the military high command assumed collectively the responsibility for the political decision to emasculate the 1967 Constitution.

When the congress was called into session by the regime in March 1970, it was a mere shadow of its former self. Of 475 legislators who took office in 1967, only 381 remained. ARENA representation dropped from 282 deputies and 46 senators to 256 deputies and 45 senators. The MDB opened the legislature with 127 deputies and 19 senators; in 1967 it had 65 deputies and 14 senators. Some legislators had died (9), some had accepted other appointments (6), and one had resigned. The others had been forcibly removed under the authority of the Institutional Acts.

The election of presiding officers indicated the consolidation of the patrimonial order. For president of the senate, ARENA selected João Cleofas de Oliveira from the Northeast state of Pernambuco. A large sugar plantation owner, Cleofas had been minister of agriculture under Vargas in the 1950s. Twice defeated for governor of his state (1954 and 1962), he returned to congress as a federal deputy and then senator (1966). The chamber president was Geraldo Freire of Minas Gerais. Also a landowner, Freire had been active in the UDN opposition to the Goulart government. A strong Catholic, he caught the eye of then War Minister Costa e Silva in 1964 when he greeted the military ministers on behalf of the UDN in a plenary session of congress. Neither man opposed the government on any issue.

The indirect gubernatorial elections of October 3, 1970, saw ARENA candidates elected in all the states except Guanabara. The MDB victory there had been ratified previously by the government. The gubernatorial candidates had been handpicked one at a time by President Médici. Gone was the old freewheeling style of state governors. The new breed was aware of its source of authority: the central government. The governors were cognizant of the group they had most to please: the military.

In the direct elections of November 1970 for a new chamber and two-thirds of the senate, ARENA won an overwhelming victory (see Table 17). Once again, congressional leadership positions were given to members of the traditional political elite, signifying the peripheral role that congress was assigned by the Médici government. Petronio Portela, former UDN governor of Piauí, became president of the senate, and UDN deputy Pereira Lopes of Sao Paulo became president of the chamber. Outgoing chamber president, Geraldo Freire, became leader of ARENA in the lower house; and Filinto Muller, Vargas's chief of police in Rio de Janeiro in the 1930s and UDN/ARENA stalwart after 1946, assumed leadership of the government party in the senate.

BRAZILIAN FOREIGN POLICY AND THE UNITED STATES

Brazil's relations with the United States must be understood from both an economic and a political perspective because the two have been, and continue to be, intertwined. In recent years there has been a growing concern about Brazil's economic dependence on the United States as well as other industrialized nations and a corresponding loss of political freedom in international affairs. The Brazilian economist Celso Furtado has written:

It is well known that the important internal political problems of Latin American countries are of direct interest to the authorities charged with the security of the United States. Likewise, the same authorities are in a position to intervene decisively in the developments of the solutions to such problems. It is therefore perfectly natural that Latin Americans inquire – with ever increasing concern – about the following: what is understood or meant within the specific context of the "security" of the United States? And how much compatibility exists between such security interests and the Latin American revolution?[6]

This theme of "external dependence" is not a new one in Latin America or in Brazil. It attained new meaning in the 1960s, and it appears that since 1964 the military regime in Brazil has determined, surprisingly perhaps, to assert Brazil's

[6] Celso Furtado, *Obstacles to Development in Latin America* (Garden City, N.Y.: Doubleday and Co., Anchor Book, 1970), p. 4.

political autonomy while simultaneously trying to lessen the country's economic dependence on the industrial nations. Thus the objective of international autonomy is a common thread that unites Brazilian foreign policy both before and after the 1964 coup. Whereas the Quadros-Goulart independent foreign policy initiative ended with the coup, the military appear willing and able to pursue a similar independence but without having to turn to the political left for support, as pre-1964 governments were forced to do.

Background

The United States and Brazil enjoyed cordial relations throughout the nineteenth century and well into the twentieth. While Getúlio Vargas maintained a wary neutrality throughout much of World War II, Brazil's Expeditionary Force, after the country's entry into the war, fought valiantly in Italy as part of the allied effort. Many of the leading military figures of the post-1945 period served in Europe and remained closely identified with the United States and its foreign policy during the Cold War. Brazil supported the United States's fierce opposition to international communist influence in the hemisphere and refused to open diplomatic relations with the Soviet Union or its satellites in Eastern Europe.

An abrupt shift came in Brazilian–United States relations with the late 1950s and early 1960s. There was lingering resentment in Brazil over the lack of support in Washington for the development recommendations made in 1952 by the Joint United States–Brazilian Economic Development Commission. Appointed during the Truman administration, its recommendations were made to the Eisenhower government, which believed that the burden of development rested with private capital and not with international public investment programs.

As well, the United States reacted less than enthusiastically to President Juscelino Kubitschek's recommendation in 1958 that the United States initiate a massive effort to improve the living standard of the people of Latin America. While Operation Pan American received little support at the time, it was an important source of the Alliance for Progress, in the opinion of many Brazilians.

Within Brazil the rising nationalism of the late 1950s pressured the government to seek a more important and independent position in world affairs and, at the same time, to oppose United States "imperialism." The left in Brazil came into its own politically at this time; its influence peaked with the Goulart years. Moreover, the import substitution policy, the foundation of Brazil's industrial efforts since 1945, had come under increasing criticism. Economic nationalists queried if it was not time to get on with full-scale economic development which would require a basic restructuring of economic and social relations in Brazil; this theme was popularized by Goulart in the 1962-64 period by his call for *Reformas da Base* — basic reforms in land tenure, taxation, vote for illiterates, and banking. As Werner Baer has written about Latin America:

By the opening of the seventies . . . there is considerable doubt about ISI's (Import Substitution Industrialization) success in solving the region's development problems. . . . the possibilities for further import substitution had disappeared. Industrial growth had slowed, job opportunities in industry . . . were scarce, income distribution . . . either remained unchanged or had become more concentrated . . . and most industrial goods produced within the region were priced so high that export possibilities were severely limited.[7]

The ISI policy of the 1950s left a legacy that the present government in Brazil is working to erase. The government's overemphasis on industrialization resulted in its neglecting the modernization of other sectors of the economy, especially agriculture. Scant attention was given to the impact on the economy of destabilizing policies such as the rapidly rising rates of inflation. Income distribution grew more unequal between regions and social groups; pressures to improve the outdated educational system grew, in order to provide a means of mobility and to train needed technicians; rising balance of payments deficits became a heavy burden on the budget. It

[7] Werner Baer, "Import Substitution Industrialization in Latin America: Experiences and Interpretations," *Latin American Research Review*, Vol. VII, No. 1 (Spring, 1972).

became clear that the country had begun to pay the price for an economic development policy that had badly neglected export promotion and production diversification.[8]

The convergence of these factors — economic slowdown, rising developmental nationalism, increasing political populism, the assertiveness of the left — coincided with the presidency of Jânio Quadros in 1961. Before his resignation in August of the same year, the government appeared to be making some headway in responding to the multiple social and political pressures demanding action. He attacked inflation, froze wages, tightened credit, and began to reorganize the government bureaucracy. In the foreign policy area, Quadros wrote that Brazil "had been relegated unjustifiably to an obscure position,"[9] but under his leadership "we preserve our absolute freedom to make our own decisions in specific cases and in the light of peaceful suggestions at one with our nature and history."[10] This "independent" or "nonaligned" foreign policy continued under João Goulart's government.

During Goulart's years in office, his support for the left and the resulting polarization of political opinion led to few reforms and a great deal of demagoguery on both sides. As the amount of profits that foreign investors could take out of the country became an issue, congress acted to restrict the remittance of profits (by 1964 United States private investment in Brazil was larger than in any other country in Latin America except for Venezuela). Three United States companies were nationalized by a state government with compensation; there were demands that mineral reserves be developed only by Brazilians and not given over to the exploitation of foreign investors.

John F. Kennedy's Alliance for Progress, promulgated in August 1961, came to Brazil's aid in 1962 after a visit by Goulart to the United States. Washington agreed to a two-year emergency impact program in the Brazilian Northeast, for $131 million, to stop the spread of communist-inspired dissension by

[8] See Werner Baer and Isaac Kerstenetsky, "The Brazilian Economy in the Sixties," in Riordan Roett (ed.), *Brazil in the Sixties* (Nashville: Vanderbilt University Press, 1972).

[9] Jânio Quadros, "Brazil's New Foreign Policy," *Foreign Affairs,* Vol. 40, No. 1 (October, 1961), 9.

[10] Ibid., p. 26.

raising the standard of living of the people; a loan agreement, negotiated between the two governments in 1963, made available $398.5 million for balance-of-payments support and as an incentive for the government to implement some of its promised reforms. Only $84 million were released as it became clear to the United States that Goulart was unwilling or unable to meet his commitments to economic and social reform. President Kennedy had canceled his proposed visit to Brazil in November 1962. A trip to Brasília by then Attorney General Robert F. Kennedy failed to convince Goulart of the United States's concern for the growing inflation. By late 1963 the United States had virtually ceased dealing with the federal government. It pursued an "island of sanity" policy — providing economic aid for those states who were able to use the money responsibly, in the American embassy's opinion.[11]

After The Coup

The 1964 coup restored amicable relations between Brasília and Washington. Foreign aid was restored; United States grants and loans accounted for about 60 percent of the $2.5 billion in United States economic assistance given to Brazil between 1962 and 1971. The other 40 percent came from Food for Peace and loans from the Export-Import Bank. The emphasis of United States aid after 1964 was on "program" loans — general support of those programs that both the Brazilians and Americans felt to be crucial for recovery— for restoration of the nation's balance-of-payments position. Since 1969 the Agency for International Development has pursued a policy of "selective sector support" — providing assistance principally in education, agricultural research, and health.

The regime's fight against inflation, combined with its success in central planning, resulted in an impressive growth record. The rate of increase in total output fell to 1.5 percent in 1963 and then rose to only 3.6 percent in the period from 1964

[11]See Peter D. Bell, "Brazilian-American Relations in the 1960's," in Riordan Roett (ed.), *Brazil in the Sixties.* Also, see the discussion in Jerome Levinson and Juan de Onis, *The Alliance that Lost Its Way* (Chicago: Quadrangle Books, 1970), especially pp. 242-53.

to 1966. By 1968 the growth rate was officially reported as 8.4 percent and about 9.0 percent in 1969 and 1970.[12]

By the early 1970s both the economic and military components of the United States foreign aid program to Brazil came under increasing criticism. Congressional hearings reflected a growing disenchantment with United States support for the Military Republic. The State Department countered congressional criticism by saying that Brazil was vital to the national interest of the United States and that, on a per capita basis, Brazil absorbed a modest amount of economic assistance in comparison to other Latin American countries, although it received the largest total amount of aid of any country in the hemisphere.[13]

As United States foreign aid to Brazil decreased, Brazil's foreign policy became increasingly independent. There was little doubt that the Military Republic would continue to be a staunch opponent of communism in the hemisphere, thus assuring a continuation of the basic compatibility between United States and Brazilian foreign policy. But in other international areas, the Brazilian government moved to recapture the Quadros spirit of independence. In international trade and economic matters, the government often was at variance with the United States. President Médici in 1970 unilaterally declared that Brazil claimed two hundred miles of the territorial sea — without prior notification to the United States, who still defended a twelve-mile limit. Brazil looked for new trading partners both in Latin America and in other areas of the world. The government has refused to sign the 1963 Nuclear Nonproliferation Treaty because it would inhibit the development of nuclear energy for peaceful purposes. Brazil's economic strength and the determination of its leadership to make Brazil a world power reflect the popular belief that

[12]*Socio-Economic Progress in Latin America,* Tenth Annual Report, 1970, of the Social Progress Trust Fund (Washington: Inter-American Development Bank, 1971), p. 130.

[13]See, for example, *United States Policies and Programs in Brazil,* Hearings before the Subcommittee on Western Hemisphere Affairs, Committee on Foreign Relations, United States Senate, 92nd Congress, 1st Session (Washington: U.S. Government Printing Office, 1971) and *Foreign Assistance and Related Programs — Appropriations for Fiscal Year 1972,* Hearings before a Subcommittee of the Committee on Appropriations, United States Senate, 92nd Congress, 1st Session (Washington: U.S. Government Printing Office, 1971).

"Brazil should be treated as an equal in the community of nations, and that her foreign policy on each issue should be determined strictly by the national interest."[14]

Brazilian–United States relations in the 1970s are bound to reflect the newfound confidence of the Military Republic in both the economic and political spheres. For the first time in Brazilian history the country is moving toward a truly independent international position. How far that autonomy will extend will be determined, in great part, by the ability of the armed forces to reorganize and reorient the Brazilian economy – implying social and economic changes that have been, thus far, inimicable to the regime – and restructure the social order. The framework they have selected, the patrimonial state, holds little promise for a structural revision of Brazilian society that would disturb established interests. To change course now would be to undermine the Military Republic itself but, possibly, would accomplish the stated goals of the 1964 "Revolution." This dilemma will occupy Brazil for this decade and beyond.

New Directions in Government Policy

As the independent foreign policy theme became clearer in the Médici administration, a new, developmental emphasis emerged in the government's domestic program, given impetus by the economic success of the later 1960s and the relative political tranquility that accompanied it. While the unity of the armed forces was by no means guaranteed, a combination of skillful administration, popular and pragmatic policies, and luck indicated that a majority of the officer corps were willing to support the Médici government's initiatives in the social and economic areas.

As part of the *Metas e Bases para A Ação de Govêrno* (Goals and Bases for Government Action), published in September, 1970, the government announced its Program of National Integration (PIN) in June of that year. The goals of the PIN, for the first phase which is to extend from 1971 to 1974, were to expand the agricultural frontier to include the Amazon Valley;

[14]Rollie E. Poppino, "Brazil's Third Government of the Revolution," *Current History,* Vol. 60, No. 354 (February, 1971), 107.

to combine the integration programs of the Northeast and the Amazon; to incorporate the population of those regions into the national economy; to create an effective program for transforming agriculture in the semiarid regions of the Northeast; to reorient the internal migration of Northeasterners toward the North and away from the overcrowded cities of the Center-South states; and to assure federal support for the industrial development of the Northeast region.

The priority projects for the first stage of the PIN were announced as (a) the construction of a highway across the Amazon and a road from Cuiabá (Mato Grosso) to Santarém (Pará); (b) a plan of large-scale colonization to accompany the road construction; and (c) the first stage of the Irrigation Plan for the Northeast, as well as a colonization program for the humid valleys of that region. The financing of the PIN came from the fiscal incentives assigned to various development agencies and programs in the two areas.

Construction of the trans-Amazon highway began immediately and quickly captured the imagination of the Brazilian people. The $500 million, 9,000-mile highway network, running two hundred miles south of the Amazon River and almost parallel to it, has been compared to the audacious construction of Brasília in the late 1950s. Protests about the danger posed to the Indian tribes in the Amazon and the long-range impact of the highway on the area's ecology have not deterred the government. Nor has criticism been acknowledged that the highway represents an escape from the reality of pressing social and economic issues elsewhere in Brazil. The highway has been termed a "fundamental part of the Plan of National Integration" by the *Jornal do Brasil* in an editorial that continued to state:

the American magazine *Time*, which in its last issue dedicated extensive coverage to the construction of the trans-Amazon highway, is correct when it mentions the pride that Brazilians feel over the opening of the nation's *new frontier*, constituted by the gigantic work of conquering and colonizing the largest empty space on the globe, the Amazon basin.[15]

Complementary programs in the overall national integra-

15"Amazonia Decifrada," *Jornal do Brasil* (Rio de Janeiro), September 11, 1971, p. 6.

tion effort, in addition to the PIN, include PROTERRA (Program of Land Redistribution and Stimulation of Agriculture and Cattle Activities in the Northeast and North) and PRODOESTE (Program for the Development of the Center-West).

The announced objectives of PROTERRA are to provide assistance to small farmers, offer greater access to the land for small cultivators, create better employment conditions, and offer support for the industrialization of agriculture in the areas under the jurisdiction of the Northeast development superintendency, SUDENE, and the Amazon development agency, SUDAM.

PRODOESTE goals are the construction of a highway network in the Center-West region, the construction of food storage facilities, sanitary improvement, land reclamation, the development and modernization of cattle raising, and the paving of the highway from Belém to Brasília.

The *Programa de Integração Social* (Program of Social Integration), first announced in August 1970, provides an opportunity for the working class to share in the national income through the Participation Fund. Both the federal government and the private sector will make contributions to the fund, from which workers will be able to draw loans for the purchase of an apartment or plot of land, etc. The extent of a worker's participation will be determined by his level of employment and length of service. A mechanism aimed at the redistribution of national income, the program will encompass the urban working class primarily.

The Social Integration Program has among its other objectives to stimulate social assistance to working-class families, expand housing and education opportunities, and increase literacy through the previously announced MOBRAL (Brazilian Literacy Movement). In large part, the Social Integration Program represents the regime's response to criticism that it has ignored the social needs of the Brazilian people since 1964 in its efforts to maintain political stability and foster economic growth.

In September 1971 President Médici sent to congress the first *Plano de Desenvolvimento Nacional* (National Development Plan), which will cover the years 1972-74. The principal goals of the Plan are to maintain annual growth rates of between 8 and 10 percent; further national integration in the Northeast and Amazon regions (as outlined in the programs discussed previously), create a modern, efficient, and technological economy; and continue planning for a higher level of social integration. The Plan projected a rise in per capita income by 1974 of more than $500 a year, and an increase in the Gross National Product sufficient to raise Brazil from ninth to eighth place among the noncommunist nations. The National Development Plan will emphasize investment in telecommunications, steel and petroleum production, naval construction, electric energy expansion, mining development, and raising the level of exports.

By 1972 the Médici regime had stated, in broad outline, its principal growth and development objectives. The welter of programs and agencies, sometimes confusing, represented the efforts of an increasingly efficient and powerful central planning apparatus. Whether the national programs proposed will be successful depends on the skill of the president in retaining sufficient military and political support and the continued momentum of the national economy.

THE FUTURE OF THE CONGRESS AND POLITICAL PARTIES

While it may be accurate to say, as Robert Packenham does, that "the maintenance of an active Congress, even if that action had little consequence for the allocation of values in Brazilian politics, was an important determinant of the legitimacy of the revolutionary regime," during the first years after the 1964 coup, it seems improbable that such was the case by 1966.[16] Packenham defines legitimation as "the production of acquiescence in, and/or support of, the moral right to rule of the government by the members of the political system (including the population at large as well as political elites)."

[16]Robert A. Packenham, "Legislatures and Political Development," in Allan Kornberg and Lloyd D. Muslof (eds.), *Legislatures in Developmental Perspective* (Durham: Duke University Press, 1970), p. 526.

The three governments of the Military Republic — the Castello Branco, Costa e Silva, and Garrastazu Médici — have all relied heavily on the 1964 Revolution itself as the source of their moral authority to rule. The Institutional Acts have explicitly stated that the March 31 movement is a continuing and permanent part of the national process of development. Specific institutions have meaning only insofar as they contribute to the maintenance of the state's preeminence in public affairs.

The military regime has made it perfectly clear that it will tolerate the congress only if the congress willingly self-abnegates any claim to an independent legislature, i.e., law-making, role. Even when the congress has fully acquiesced, momentary rebellions, such as those in 1966 and 1968, have brought down the heavy hand of military/state power. The minor legitimatizing function of the Brazilian congress in 1964-65 is far outweighed by the lack of protest from political elites or popular classes over the reduction in influence of the legislature.

To play a legitimatizing role, an institution must, itself, be viewed as legitimate. There is little, if any, evidence that congress, at any time in Brazilian history, has been considered to exercise legitimate authority in national politics. There have been too few instances when congress had the opportunity of exercising an influential role in policy-making. The 1946 Republic was possibly one such time. But given the fragility of the representative political system and the inclinative nature of the party system, the congress never achieved a high degree of legitimacy in the eyes of the elite or the mass. For the latter it was a barrier to the fulfillment of campaign promises; to the former it was a vehicle for self-aggrandizement and personal influence.

The military regime treated the congress with such disdain precisely because it had not achieved a position of legitimacy in the 1946 Republic. They saw it as a necessary evil; necessary because its functioning maintained the fiction of democratic government that has characterized all Brazilian regimes; an evil because it harbored the most prominent, and suspect, servants of the old order. For the military it was better to tolerate and emasculate the congress than to shut it out completely.

Reporting on his survey of Brazilian representative associations to determine how often they made contact with authority groups and other institutions, Philippe Schmitter reports that "among government organs, the concentration of attention upon federal administrative agencies is most marked." He continues that "evidence from a variety of sources indicates that association leaders see the legislature as a target of only secondary significance." And, "the most striking (but not unanticipated) finding concerns political parties: 72.4 percent report that they never have any contact with parties, and another 13.8 percent have had only rare contact."[17]

Schmitter's data supports our analysis that the congress and political party system have little, if any, political significance in Brazil in the policy-making arena. The military governments have been able to deal as severely as they have with these institutions because of their irrelevance to other groups in society. The lack of credibility possessed by these institutions has facilitated the military's hold over the patrimonial state.

Another indication of the growing power of the patrimonial regime can be gained from an examination of the data gathered on public and private investment by Andrea Maneschi (see Table 18). The military regime has continued the corporatist emphasis apparent during the preceding decades. Maneschi's data demonstrate the growing economic influence of a regime with a heavy preponderance of political power. The institutionalization of power has been accompanied by an increase in the size of the bureaucracy: the instrument for policy formation both before and after March 1964 (see Figure 1). The military regime has done nothing to reduce the speed of public control. On the contrary, with no effective opposition from parties, congress, interest groups, or social units, the armed forces have been able to consolidate the patrimonial state more efficiently and effectively, for their purposes, than has any preceding regime.

CONCLUSION

In perspective the Military Republic should be seen as a logical culmination of the neodemocratic chaos of the 1946-64

[17]Schmitter, *Interest Conflict,* pp. 257-61.

Table 18
PUBLIC AND PRIVATE INVESTMENT SHARES
AND SECTORAL PARTICIPATION
IN GOVERNMENT ENTERPRISE INVESTMENT, 1947-65
(percentages)

Years	$\frac{GI}{TI}$	$\frac{GEI}{TI}$	$\frac{PEI}{TI}$	Sectoral Participation in GEI					
				Mining	Iron & Steel	Chemicals	Power	Transport	Other
1947-50	23.3	2.6	74.1	17.5	23.1	0.8	7.1	13.7	37.8
1951-55	20.2	3.0	76.8	4.0	34.1	24.2	11.9	5.2	20.7
1956-60	25.5	7.8	66.7	4.5	9.0	36.9	11.3	26.2	11.9
1961-63	24.4	13.1	62.5	3.9	40.3	17.3	12.7	17.2	8.7
1964-65	27.6	12.9	59.5	5.2	38.0	21.7	16.7	10.7	7.7
1960	27.1	11.6	61.3	6.3	15.3	38.2	13.0	13.3	13.9
1961	24.8	14.4	60.7	3.1	42.1	17.1	8.9	16.3	12.4
1962	25.2	13.5	61.3	3.6	49.9	14.5	9.5	16.4	6.2
1963	23.3	11.4	65.4	5.3	26.2	20.8	21.4	19.2	7.1
1964	25.4	9.4	65.3	4.6	24.8	24.3	23.8	13.5	9.0
1965	29.9	16.5	53.6	5.6	45.7	20.2	12.6	9.0	6.9

Source: Andrea Maneschi, "The Brazilian Public Sector During the Sixties," in Riordan Roett (ed.) *Brazil in the Sixties* (Nashville: Vanderbilt University Press, 1972).

Symbols: TI = total gross fixed investment
 GI = government gross fixed investment
 GEI = government enterprise gross fixed investment
 PEI = private enterprise gross fixed investment

era. The institutional development of the patrimonial state had not produced the procedures needed to reconcile the conflicting demands made on the political system. When it became apparent that public order was in jeopardy and that the groups lobbying for radical social and economic reform were willing to destroy the basic institutions of the patrimonial regime, the military exercised the right to intervene that they had acquired in 1889.

The Military Republic has demonstrated how inapplicable the pluralist democratic model is to Brazil. Neither historical precedent nor social pressure provides any justification for its adaptation by Brazilian political elites. The "givens" of our introductory chapter are applicable to the 1970s as they have been to the preceding decades. The ease with which the military assumed and exercised power in 1964, without sustained and

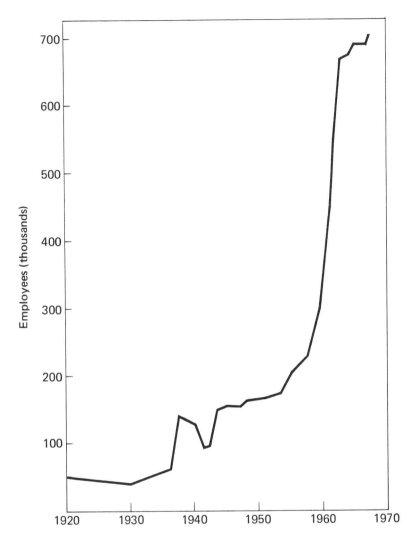

Figure 1. EMPLOYMENT IN FEDERAL GOVERNMENT, 1920-70.

Source: Philippe C. Schmitter, *Interest Conflict and Political Change in Brazil* (Stanford: Stanford University Press, 1971), p. 33.

debilitating opposition, indicates that the patrimonial model of co-option and cooperation will continue to be applicable to

Brazil. Such a model does not foreclose economic growth or social mobility, as long as these take place within generally understood "rules of the game."

To predict that the Military Republic will continue to exercise and monopolize political power in Brazil is neither to sanction nor to condemn such a development. Such a prediction emanates from an analysis of Brazilian development, hopefully factual and objective. The study of Brazil clearly indicates that there are various paths to change in the Third World. The pluralist democratic and totalitarian provide only two examples, neither particularly relevant to Latin America. The patrimonial regime concept has wider application to all of Latin America, as Claudio Veliz emphasizes in writing that "the politics of conformity which have dominated the last decade have apparently led to the return of a paternalistic centralism which has a great deal in common with the traditions of the Spanish Enlightenment."[18] That a convergence between the Portuguese and Spanish traditions in Latin America may be taking place has been noted by Ronald Schneider: "although historically the Brazilian system has differed from the Hispanic authoritarian model quite sharply on the dimension of mobilization, this divergence has been greatly reduced since 1965 and particularly since December, 1968."[19]

Given the weakness of social groups and the strong tradition of patrimonialism in Brazil, the internal dynamics of the armed forces may well provide the greatest insights into the country's political future. Seemingly unconcerned with mass political parties, representative institutions, or the organization of the countryside as a means of insuring stability, the military views the 1970s with guarded optimism. Determined to modernize on the basis of previous economic growth, confident that the social initiatives of the regime will be sufficient to absorb popular discontent, and hopeful that a heterogeneous officer corps will see more value in accepting and supporting the third government of the "Revolution" than in overthrowing it, the Garrastazu Médici government expects to prepare the nation for the tenth anniversary of the March 31 coup d'état. Based on

[18] Claudio Veliz, "Introduction," in Claudio Veliz (ed.), *The Politics of Conformity in Latin America* (New York: Oxford University Press, 1967), pp. 12-13.
[19] Schneider, *The Political System of Brazil*, p. 346.

our present evaluation of the Brazilian political system, the only group that will be able to supplant the incumbent military regime would be another faction of the armed forces, desirous not of a more open political system but rather of a greater institutionalization of the patrimonial order in contemporary Brazil.

SELECTED BIBLIOGRAPHY

The books and articles included in this selected bibliography emphasize the period since 1945 — covering the 1946 Republic and its successor, the Military Republic. I have chosen works that deal with the political system in general or with those parts of it that I have examined in this book. The list is not meant to be exhaustive, since it excludes many items in English and offers no guidance to the literature in Portuguese. In addition, important works in English, such as Robert Levine, *The Vargas Regime: The Critical Years, 1934-1938* (New York and London: Columbia University Press, 1970); Warren Dean, *The Industrialization of São Paulo, 1880-1945* (Austin and London: University of Texas Press, 1969); Charles Wagley, *An Introduction to Brazil*, revised edition (New York and London: Columbia University Press, 1971); and Werner Baer, *Industrialization and Economic Development in Brazil* (Homewood, Ill.: Richard D. Irwin, 1965), to name only a few from other social science disciplines, should be consulted for a more comprehensive understanding of the modernization process in Brazil in the twentieth century.

Books

Baklanoff, Eric N., (ed.). *New Perspectives of Brazil.* Nashville: Vanderbilt University Press, 1966.
    A multidisciplinary collection of essays that seeks to explore the complexity of Brazil's development.

_____ . *The Shaping of Modern Brazil.* Baton Rouge: Louisiana State University Press, 1969.
    A collection of short, introductory papers that consider "a number of critical variables and processes that have shaped contemporary Brazil — intellectual, social, political, economic, and geographic."

Bello, José Maria. *A History of Modern Brazil, 1889-1964.* Stanford: Stanford University Press, 1966. Translated from the Portuguese by James L. Taylor with a new concluding chapter by Rollie E. Poppino.
    A standard history by a pre-1930 member of the political elite with a good concluding chapter by Professor Poppino.

Burns, E. Bradford. *Nationalism in Brazil: A Historical Survey.* New York:

Frederick A. Praeger, 1968.
A useful introduction to an important subject: "nationalism promises to liberate Brazil from the past and to propel it into the future."

Daland, Robert G. *Brazilian Planning: Development Politics and Administration.* Chapel Hill: The University of North Carolina Press, 1967. Very competent analysis of planning and politics in a country "which has a twenty-year history of conscious, institutionalized, central planning."

Dougherty, Charles, Rowe, James W., and Schneider, Ronald M. *Brazil Election Factbook, No. 2.* Washington, D.C.: Institute for the Comparative Study of Political Systems, 1965.
An updating of the earlier *Factbook* to include the 1965 elections.

Dulles, John W. F. *Vargas of Brazil: A Political Biography.* Austin and London: University of Texas Press, 1967.
A somewhat journalistic account but all there is in English to date on Brazil's most important political leader in the twentieth centry.

————. *Unrest in Brazil: Political-Military Crises, 1955-1964.* Austin and London: University of Texas Press, 1969.
Helpful information on an important ten-year period that preceded the coup d'état of March 31, 1964.

Einaudi, Luigi R., and Stepan, Alfred C., III. *Latin American Institutional Development: Changing Military Perspectives in Peru and Brazil.* A report prepared for the Office of External Research, Department of State. Santa Monica, Cal.: The RAND Corporation, 1971.
"This report traces the evolution, and analyzes some of the implications, of the ways in which the military forces in Peru and Brazil see the issues of national security and foreign policy in their respective countries."

Free, Lloyd. *Some International Implications of the Political Psychology of Brazilians.* Princeton, N.J.: Institute for International Social Research, 1961.
Good background material for the 1960s on political attitudes and beliefs.

Graham, Lawrence S. *Civil Service Reform in Brazil: Principles versus Practice.* Austin and London: University of Texas Press, 1968. Published for the Institute of Latin American Studies.
"The purpose of this study is to analyze the Brazilian experience with reform of its federal civil service and to demonstrate the interrelationship between the ideas and concepts on which the reform movement has been based and the political context within which the federal civil service has operated."

Hirschman, Albert O. *Journeys Toward Progress: Studies of Economic Policy-Making in Latin America.* New York: The Twentieth Century Fund, 1963. Esp. chapter 1, "Brazil's Northeast," pp. 11-92.

Ianni, Octavio. *Crisis in Brazil.* New York: Columbia University Press, 1970. Published originally as *O Colapso do Populismo no Brasil.* Rio de Janeiro: Civilização Brasileira, 1968.
An exploration of populism as a political model for development in a mass society.

Institute for the Comparative Study of Political Systems. *Brazil Election Factbook No. 1.* Washington, D.C.: Institute for the Comparative Study of Political Systems, 1962.
A very useful source of electoral and political background data.

———. *Brazil Election Factbook No. 2, Supplement.* Washington, D.C.: Institute for the Comparative Study of Political Systems, 1966.

Jaguaribe, Hélio. *Economic and Political Development: A Theoretical Approach and a Brazilian Case Study.* Cambridge: Harvard University Press, 1968.
An updated (through 1966) and revised translation of the first Brazilian edition published in 1962. The volume, by one of Brazil's best-known political scientists, deals with "the problems involved in the deliberate promotion of national development and with a general theory of political models" and offers a case study of Brazil.

Johnson, John J. *The Military and Society in Latin America.* Stanford: Stanford University Press, 1964. Esp. Part III, "The Military in Brazil."
A good historical summary, to 1964, of the strongest interest group in Brazilian society, the military.

Kadt, Emanuel de. *Catholic Radicals in Brazil.* London and New York: Oxford University Press, 1970. Issued under the auspices of the Royal Institute of International Affairs.
A successful "attempt to throw some light on the ideas and activities of that small minority among Brazil's committed Catholics who could be called 'radicals' in the social and political spheres." The author's case study is the Movement for Basic Education, MEB.

Kahl, Joseph A. *The Measurement of Modernism: A Study of Values in Brazil and Mexico.* Austin and London: The University of Texas Press, 1968.
A comparative monograph that summarizes a study of traditional and modern values carried out in the early 1960s. The author's principal concern is "to what degree does industrialism create a common way of life for all peoples?"

Leff, Nathaniel. *Economic Policy-Making and Development in Brazil, 1947-1964.* New York: John Wiley & Son, 1968.
"This is a study of the effects of politics on economic policy and economic development in Brazil." The first part examines what was done in specific areas of Brazilian economic policy; in the second, the author discusses the politics of economic policy in postwar Brazil.

Reisky de Dubnic, Vladimir. *Political Trends in Brazil.* Washington, D.C.:

Public Affairs Press, 1968.
An introduction to some aspects of Brazilian politics, particularly political parties and foreign policy.

Richardson, Ivan L. (ed.). *Perspectives of Brazilian State and Local Government.* Los Angeles: International Public Administration Center, School of Public Administration, University of Southern California, 1965.
Considerations of local and state government that offer both new information and a helpful summary of existing knowledge.

Robock, Stefan H. *Brazil's Developing Northeast: A Study of Regional Planning and Foreign Aid.* Washington, D.C.: Brookings Institution, 1963.
An examination of the issues of development planning and foreign aid in the Brazilian Northeast before March 31, 1964. The author was optimistic about the future of the region when this book was written.

Rodrigues, José Honório. *The Brazilians: Their Character and Aspirations.* Austin: University of Texas Press, 1968. Originally published as *Aspiracois Nacionais: Interpretação Histórico-Político.* São Paulo: Editôra Fulgor, 1963.
An attempt to analyze Brazil's political culture through an analysis of national aspirations.

Roett, Riordan. *The Politics of Foreign Aid in the Brazilian Northeast.* Nashville: Vanderbilt University Press, 1972.
The author focuses on the political impact of United States foreign aid in the Northeast through an analysis of the relationship between the Development Superintendency for the Northeast (SUDENE) and the United States Agency for International Development.

———. (ed.). *Brazil in the Sixties.* Nashville: Vanderbilt University Press, 1972.
A collection of multidisciplinary essays, published here for the first time, dealing with aspects of Brazilian modernization in the crucial decade of the 1960s.

Schmitter, Philippe C. *Interest Conflict and Political Change in Brazil.* Stanford: Stanford University Press, 1971.
A scholarly and exciting effort to demonstrate empirically Tocqueville's "law" about "the art of associating together" and "to link systematically the concepts and hypotheses of interest group theory and those of political development." The author's hypotheses are tested in the light of the Brazilian experience from 1930 to 1965.

Schneider, Ronald M. *The Political System of Brazil: Emergence of A "Modernizing" Authoritarian Regime, 1964-1970.* New York and London: Columbia University Press, 1971.
Thorough and exhaustive, this study of "the emerging political system since 1964" will be followed by a second volume on the 1889-1964 period. The focus of this volume "is the systems

boundary change catalyzed by the April, 1964, replacement of a populist, albeit essentially reconciliationist, regime by the military's first experience with direct exercise of governmental authority and political power since the 1889-1894 period."

Sherwood, Frank P. *Institutionalizing the Grass Roots in Brazil: A Study in Comparative Local Government.* San Francisco: Chandler Publishing Co., 1967.
An informative discussion of a topic little discussed in the English literature on Brazil — "the problem of creating and retaining effective, representative, and dynamic political institutions at the local level. . . ."

Skidmore, Thomas E. *Politics in Brazil, 1930-1964: An Experiment in Democracy.* New York: Oxford University Press, 1967.
The author has written "an interpretation of what I regard as the most important factors determining the trend of Brazilian politics since the Revolution of 1930." A well-written exposition of Brazil's political history with balanced analysis, from 1930 to 1964.

Stepan, Alfred. *The Military in Politics: Changing Patterns in Brazil.* Princeton: Princeton University Press, 1971.
An excellent analysis of the role of the military in Brazilian politics.

Wiarda, Howard J. *The Brazilian Catholic Labor Movement.* Amherst, Mass.: University of Massachusetts Labor Relations and Research Center, 1969.
A concise and useful investigation of the obstacles to the growth of the Brazilian labor movement.

Wirth, John D. *The Politics of Brazilian Development, 1930-1954.* Stanford: Stanford University Press, 1970.
"This book is a study of policy-making during the long Vargas era (1930-1954) when the basic decisions to industrialize were taken. It analyzes three case studies of foreign trade, steel, and petroleum. . . ." A good addition to our knowledge of the post-1930 period.

Young, Jordan M. *The Brazilian Revolution of 1930 and the Aftermath.* New Brunswick, N.J.: Rutgers University Press, 1967.
A consideration "of some of the hard political facts that went into the planning, maneuvering and execution of the successful 1930 revolt" that brought Getúlio Vargas to power.

Articles

Blume, Norman. "Pressure Groups and Decision-Making in Brazil." *Studies in Comparative International Development* 3, No. 11 (1968). St. Louis, Mo.: Social Science Institute, Washington University.
Considers the interrelationship of the presidency, the legislature, the administrative agencies, and the courts and pressure groups.

Bonilla, Frank. "A National Ideology for Development: Brazil." pp. 232-264 in K.H. Silvert (ed.), *Expectant Peoples: Nationalism and Development*. New York: Random House, 1963.
A balanced, informed treatment of nationalism in Brazil before 1964.

_____. "Brazil," pp. 195-221 in James Coleman (ed.), *Education and Political Development*. Princeton: Princeton University Press, 1965.
A perceptive analysis of the Brazilian educational system and its role in political development.

Busey, James L. "Brazil's Reputation for Political Stability." *Western Political Quarterly* 18, No. 4 (December, 1965): 866-80.

Daland, Robert T. "Development Administration and the Brazilian Political System." *Western Political Quarterly* 21, No. 2 (June, 1968): 325-39.
Using Riggs's model, the author carefully explores the hypothesis that "a prismatic political system which is characterized by a non-consensual elite and a history of systemic instability, can achieve optimum governmental participation in national development only through decentralization of development-oriented programs."

Evans, Robert D. "The Brazilian Revolution of 1964: Political Surgery Without Anaesthetics." *International Affairs* (London) 44, No. 2 (April, 1968): 267-81.
A basically descriptive summary of the major events surrounding the 1964 military intervention.

Furtado, Celso. "Political Obstacles to Economic Growth in Brazil," pp. 145-61 in Claudio Veliz (ed.), *Obstacles to Change in Latin America*. New York: Oxford University Press, 1965.
A concise summary of the obstacles to development that Brazil has confronted.

Harding, Timothy F. "Revolution Tomorrow: The Failure of the Left in Brazil," *Studies on the Left* 6, No. 4 (Fall, 1964): 43-52.
A probing consideration of why the Left failed to unite and achieve its political goals.

Hewitt, Cynthia N. "Brazil: The Peasant Movement of Pernambuco, 1961-1964," pp. 374-98 in Henry A. Landsberger (ed.), *Latin American Peasant Movements*. Ithaca and London: Cornell University Press, 1969.
The ideological and organizational complexities of the peasant movement in the Northeast in the early 1960s is ably summarized here.

Jaguaribe, Hélio. "The Dynamics of Brazilian Nationalism," pp. 162-187 in Claudio Veliz (ed.), *Obstacles to Change in Latin America*. New York: Oxford University Press, 1965.
The author repeats his theme of the cartorial ("sinecure") state in considering development and nationalism.

Kadt, Emanuel de. "Religion, the Church, and Social Change in Brazil," pp. 192-220 in Claudio Veliz (ed.), *The Politics of Conformity in Latin America.* New York: Oxford University Press, 1967.
A well-argued summary of the Church, its policies, the challenge of Spiritualism and Messianism, and the future of progressive reform.

Leeds, Anthony. "Brazil and the Myth of Francisco Julião," pp. 190-204 in Joseph Maier and Richard W. Weatherhead (eds.), *Politics of Change in Latin America.* New York: Frederick A. Praeger, 1964.
An insightful treatment of an intriguing phenomenon — Julião and the Peasant Leagues in the Northeast. The author concludes that Julião represented a continuation of, and not a break with, traditional forms of political leadership.

Moraes, Clodomir. "Peasant Leagues in Brazil," pp. 453-502 in Rodolfo Stavenhagen (ed.), *Agrarian Problems and Peasant Movements in Latin America.* Garden City, N.Y.: Doubleday & Co., Anchor Books, 1970.
A sympathetic treatment of peasant activism in Brazil, comparing the Peasant Leagues and the Communist Party-inspired Union of Laborers and Agricultural Workers of Brazil (ULTAB).

Morse, Richard M. "Some Themes of Brazilian History." *The South Atlantic Quarterly* 61 (Spring, 1962): 159-82.
A clear and useful summary of recurring themes in Brazil's historical development.

Myhr, Robert O. "Brazil," in Donald K. Emerson (ed.), *Student Politics in Developing Nations.* New York: Frederick A. Praeger, 1968.
One of the best summary pieces in English on the student movement.

_____. "Nationalism in the Brazilian Student Movement." *Inter-American Economic Affairs* 22, No. 4 (Spring, 1969): 89-94.

_____. "The University Student Tradition in Brazil." *Journal of Inter-American Studies and World Affairs* 12, No. 1 (January, 1970): 126-40.

Peterson, Phyllis. "Coalition Formation in Local Elections in the State of São Paulo, Brazil," pp. 141-59 in Sven Groennings et al., *The Study of Coalition Behavior: Theoretical Perspectives and Cases from Four Continents.* New York: Holt, Rinehart and Winston, 1970.
A fascinating look at "the process of coalition formation in one segment of (an) unstable system . . . in local elections in the state of São Paulo, Brazil."

_____. "Brazil: Revolution or Reaction?" pp. 516-74 in Martin C. Needler (ed.), *Political Systems of Latin America*, 2nd ed. New York: Van Nostrand Reinhold Company, 1970.
The author provides a well-written summary review of the political system.

Richardson, Ivan L. "Municipal Government in Brazil: The Financial Dimension." *Journal of Comparative Administration* 1, No. 3 (November, 1969).
A helpful article on finanaces and local government problems in Brazil.

Rowe, James W. "Revolution or Counterrevolution in Brazil? Part I: The Diverse Background" and "Part II: From Black Tuesday to the New Reform," *American Universities Field Staff Reports*, East Coast South America Series, 11, Nos. 4 and 5 (June, 1964).
"The 'Revolution' and the 'System': Notes on Brazilian Politics, Part I: Seeds of the System,"; "Part II: The 'System' — Full Flower and Crisis"; and "Part III: The 'Revolution' — Generals and Technocrats," *American Universities Field Staff Reports*, East Coast South America Series, 12, Nos. 3, 4, and 5 (July-August, 1966); and "Brazil Stops the Clock, Part I: 'Democratic Formalism' before 1964 and in the Election of 1966," and "Part II: The New Constitution and the New Model," *American Universities Field Staff Reports*, East Coast South America Series, 13, Nos. 1 and 2 (March, 1967).
An excellent series of reports on politics and the political system before and after March 31, 1964.

Sanders, Thomas G. "Catholicism and Development: The Catholic Left in Brazil," pp. 81-100 in Kalman H. Silvert (ed.), *Churches and States: The Religious Institution and Modernization.* New York: American Universities Field Staff, 1967.
A penetrating evaluation of the Catholic Left, "an elitist movement within the divided Brazilian Church that responded in a serious and radical way to pressures within society for economic development and social change."

Siegel, Gilbert B. "The Strategy of Public Administration Reform: The Case of Brazil." *Public Administration Review* 26, No. 1 (March, 1966): 45-55.
The primary purpose is to provide a case study of a centralized staff agency — the Administrative Department of the Public Service (DASP) — and its failure.

Soares, Glaucio Ary Dillon. "The New Industrialization and the Brazilian Political System," pp. 186-201 in James Petras and Maurice Zeitlin (eds.), *Latin America: Reform or Revolution?* New York: Fawcett, 1968.
The author believes "that it is only a matter of time until the working class starts offering a mass response to revolutionary appeals . . . as it perceives its socioeconomic problems as political in nature and as the 'government' is seen as the institution that may solve these problems."

————. "The Politics of Uneven Development: The Case of Brazil," pp. 467-96 in Seymour M. Lipset and Stein Rokkan (eds.), *Party Systems and Voter Alignments: Cross-National Perspectives.* New

York: The Free Press, 1967.

The central aim of this thought-provoking essay is "to relate regional differences in Brazilian politics with underlying socio-economic differences."

Wedge, Bryant. "The Case Study of Student Political Violence: Brazil, 1964 and Dominican Republic, 1965." *World Politics* 21, No. 2 (January, 1969): 183-206.

The Brazilian case "suggests that where the preconditions for violence have only moderate force there is considerable tolerance for provocative incidents."

Weffort, Francisco C. "State and Mass in Brazil." *Studies in Comparative International Development* 2, No. 12 (1966): 187-96. St. Louis, Mo.: Social Science Institute, Washington University.

A helpful summary of the author's valuable work on political populism in post-1945 Brazil.

INDEX